MW01065044

FUTURE
CAPABLE
COMPANY

What Manufacturing Leaders Need to Do Today to Succeed Tomorrow

James A. Tompkins, Ph.D.

TOMPKINS
PRESS

Library of Congress Cataloging-in-Publication Data

Tompkins, James A.
   Future capable company: what manufacturing leaders need to do today to succeed tomorrow / James A. Tompkins. -- 1st ed.
      p. cm.
      Includes index.
      LCCN: 2001130582
      ISBN: 1-930426-01-1

   1. Production management.   I. Title.

TS155.T66 2001   658.5
                           QBI01-200880

CONTENTS

Acknowledgements

This book would not have been possible without the help of many, many people whose support was invaluable. I would like to thank:

- Tompkins Associates clients around the world who continue to have confidence in our abilities to push the envelope of innovation to achieve great results;
- Tompkins technical ranks including Mike Futch, Dale Harmelink, Rob Haynes, Bill Mattel, Denny McKnight, Pete Peters, Jerry Smith, and John Spain;
- Tompkins Press including Forsyth Alexander, Ron Gallagher, Josh Grinstead, Brenda Jernigan, Pam King, Sue Liggio, Debra Luhring, Scheryl Schonauer, and Kami Spangenberg; and
- My family who continues to be patient as I bang away at presenting to others the science of Total Operations that I have had the privilege to learn.

FOREWORD

In 1988, Jim Tompkins wrote a book called *Winning Manufacturing*. Thirteen years later, it is still selling. Manufacturers all over the world still refer to it. In fact, it is one of the five best-selling manufacturing books in print today.

So much has changed since he wrote that book. Today we live in a world of instant communication and constant change. To compete, a company must understand how its manufacturing operation is synthesized with its supply chain because as Jim Tompkins notes, companies no longer compete, in our world, supply chains do. Guided by his vision for supply chain success, Jim updated the material and expanded the scope of *Winning Manufacturing* to give us *Future Capable Company*.

Del Kimbler, in his preface to *Winning Manufacturing*, said "This book presents a sound approach to achieving manufacturing success. This book will make a real difference in your manufacturing operation." If he were writing a preface to the *Future Capable Company*, I think he would say, "This book presents a sound approach to achieving supply chain success. This book will make a real difference as your organization pursues supply chain excellence."

In hearing what company leaders have said to Jim over the past 13 years regarding how much *Winning Manufacturing* has enhanced their manufacturing excellence, I have no doubt that 13 years from now, we'll be sharing those same stories about how *Future Capable Company* changed their perspective and transformed their supply chain operations.

Jerry D. Smith
Senior Partner
Tompkins Associates

PREFACE

Today's world is so different that I never stop being amazed when I look at what's happened since I wrote *Winning Manufacturing*. Perhaps the most striking occurrence in my world, other than the advancement of technology and the advent of the Internet, has been the strengthening of the supply chain to the point where competition is no longer company vs. company, but supply chain vs. supply chain. To succeed in this new world, a company must be capable of transforming its supply chain and embracing the future to achieve success. I see this company as future capable, hence the Future Capable Company.

None of us can rest on our laurels. Success often begets failure unless we focus beyond the first peak of success to the next peak and the peak after that. In 2000, I took a look at the peak beyond *Winning Manufacturing* and I saw the *Future Capable Company*. Therefore, I decided to take the principles and Requirements of Success in *Winning Manufacturing* and adapt them to the *Future Capable Company*. I soon realized that some things never change, no matter what the millennium. To achieve success and competitive advantage, companies must reduce costs, minimize process failures, globalize, and improve quality. Therefore, those requirements, first introduced in 1988, are still requirements of success in the 21st century. I then took the rest and updated them, with two of my other books, *Revolution* and *No Boundaries,* as reference. The result is the following 12 Requirements of Success for the Future Capable Company, an interesting parallel, since it has been 12 years since I wrote *Winning Manufacturing*:

1. Cost
2. Customer Satisfaction—an expansion of Manufacturing and

Marketing
3. Global
4. Speed—a combination of Lead Times and Production Lot Sizes
5. Certainty/Change (a combination of Uncertainty and Adaptability)
6. Control—a combination and expansion of Production and Inventory Control, Material Flow, Material Tracking and Control, and Simplification
7. Balance—a combination of Balance and Inventories
8. Quality
9. Maintenance
10. Human Capital—an expansion of Human Resources
11. Continuous Improvement—an expansion of Team Players
12. Synthesis—a combination of Integration and Understanding

These requirements, addressed robustly, will mean competitive advantage for your organization and set you on the path to supply chain excellence.

So, I say to you: Become a Future Capable Company and make a real difference in your supply chain operations. Use this book as your guide. It will be as useful to today's organization as *Winning Manufacturing* has been for the past 13 years.

James A. Tompkins, Ph.D.
Raleigh, North Carolina
June, 2001

jtompkins@tompkinsinc.com

INTRODUCTION

"The times, they are changin'." When Bob Dylan sang that song, it was the 1960s. However, the line is as appropriate today as it was then, perhaps even more so. There are changes in the way we manufacture products, the way our customers shop, and the way we do business. Many of these changes can be attributed to the Internet. These changes are coming so fast and so furiously that we can no longer make assumptions about what is happening or what will happen next. It is possible to feel lost in this rapid-fire, constantly evolving business environment. But, it is also possible to chart a course direct to success. The company that will succeed in this environment is the Future Capable Company.

The Future Capable Company is a manufacturing company that responds to the forces of change while using the proper application of technology. It not only focuses on the best solutions for today's requirements, it also focuses on the solution after the next solution and moves from peak to peak to peak. The Future Capable Company harnesses the power of change while integrating all operations and applying technology for today's as well as tomorrow's requirements. It adapts, builds, and redesigns plants, uses lean production principles, makes sure its workers are IT-savvy and using best practices, and remembers that satisfying the customer should be the goal of the entire supply chain.

How does a company become a Future Capable Company? The answers to that question may be found in this book. It will provide you with the information and tools needed to transform your company and put it firmly on the Future Capable Company Path to Success. GO! GO! GO!

chapter 1

Manufacturing Today

F rom the 1950s to the 1970s, science fiction films showed us a future filled with rocket ships traveling to distant planets. The writers of that time felt that with the growth of the space program, space was where our future lay. Other than Arthur C. Clarke, the creator of Hal, most analysts and writers of that day regarded computers as huge mainframes that rattled and whirred in the backrooms of office buildings, if they thought of computers at all. They certainly did not think they would have much impact on the future. It was all rockets and warfare.

What a difference a generation makes! At the end of the 1970s and the beginning of the 1980s, computers began to infiltrate everyday living. There were scanners in grocery stores and personal computers on the desks of many workers. Software began to appear in factories and warehouses around the world to keep track of inventory and to handle planning and scheduling.

In 1969, the U.S. government created ARPANET, which eventually became the "Internet." In 1994, the Internet had more than 200 million users and has since been growing at an estimated rate of 25 percent per month. Four years before that, in 1990, Tim Berners-Lee proposed an Internet-based hypermedia initiative for global information sharing to CERN, the European Laboratory for Particle Physics. He called this initiative the "World Wide Web," and it has evolved from an advertising medium to a place for dialogue, relationships, business transactions, sales, and supply chain visibility.

So, now we travel in space, but it's cyberspace, not rocket trips sponsored by NASA. Personal and networked computers, the Internet, and the World Wide Web have changed everything. We are all connected and information is instantaneous. This has blurred and eliminated boundaries so that today's marketplaces are no longer restricted to a country or two, but are global, reaching new customers everyday.

Because of these developments, companies can no longer focus solely on creating the best and highest-value products; they must make sure the products are being created with the ability to be customized to meet as-yet-undefined customer requirements, being produced at low cost and high quality while maintaining speed and nimbleness. They must become Future Capable companies, responding to the forces of change while using the proper application of technology. To understand how this is done, let's take a closer look at change and how it is affecting us.

CHANGE: ALL ASSUMPTIONS ARE WRONG

Everything will change, and I mean everything! Even change is changing!

Changes are coming too fast and furiously for anyone to grab onto for any length of time. Companies must establish strategies that will be sufficiently flexible and modular to meet the requirements of the future, even though future requirements cannot be clearly defined. Today's customer-centric and global business environment simply does not allow us to blindly accept assumptions because all assumptions at some point will be wrong.

People and technology are the two primary drivers of change. People are driving change because there are so many of us now. Not only is the world growing, but it is growing at an increasingly rapid rate. There are more countries and more products, creating fragmentation—a marketplace broken into small segments. At the same time, the world's economy is no longer driven by capital; instead it is driven by knowledge. In some cases, the focus is no longer value-added, but knowledge-added.

CHANGE

Change is not obscure, hidden, or mysterious. It's everywhere.

- In 1956, there were 7,000 periodicals published in the United States. Today, there are more than 22,000.
- In 1989, the average supermarket stocked 25,000 items. Today, there are more than 30,000 items.
- From 1892 to 1982, there was only one Coke. Today, there are seven varieties.
- In today's automobile, the microelectronics cost more dollars than the steel.
- When I was a boy, you could either buy tennis shoes or basketball shoes. By 1990, you could buy tennis, basketball, running, walking, aerobic and cross-training styles. Today, one company sells 10 versions of its walking shoes, including one for walking just uphill.
- Someone who wanted to buy running shoes in 1970 might have found five styles from which to choose. Today, there are 300 to consider.

People's attitudes are also changing. More and more of us are yearning for a greater purpose. Books on values, virtues, and spirituality are bestsellers. Our social contracts are still based on loyalty, but our commitments may be virtual. Many consider the benefits of being self-employed.

Meanwhile, technology has been exploding even more rapidly than the population. Consider computer power. Today, there is more computer power in your car than in the first manned spacecraft. Today's home video camera has more power than the IBM 360. My own PC has more power than all the computer power on Earth in 1950.

The Web is the most noticeable instrument in the change that has occurred in the last two decades, not only because it has grown so quickly, but because it is becoming so widely used. On the Web, buyers can easily compare products, prices, and services, as well as communicate with far more people than they have in the past. New relationships are forged daily and, when they are vendor-customer relationships, the playing field is leveled, reducing the value of branding and accelerating margin pressures. The importance of providing quality service and high levels of customer satisfaction becomes paramount.

Other advancements, such as digital and wireless technologies, have changed the methods of doing business. Thanks to these technologies, corporate power has shifted from within the company to outside the company. Customers are offered a wide range of choices and can shift from one option to another almost instantly.

The explosion of both population and technology has also introduced major changes in workplaces and work processes. For example, factories may now be focused factories or even virtual factories. A focused factory is defined around a product family that requires similar manufacturing equipment. In other words, it is specialized rather than generalized. Virtual factories are virtual enterprises that gather, organize, select, synthesize, and distribute information and parts with information technology, be it Electronic Data Interchange (EDI), wireless, the Internet, or a combination of all three.

Also, direct-to-consumer delivery channels, customer satisfaction, customization, shorter cycle and lead-times, cellular and flow manufacturing, and small lot sizes are emphasized as more and more companies and customers look to the Web for products and information for the entire supply chain. As a result, Build-to-Order (BTO) is being viewed as a viable alternative to mass production, which cannot provide the speed and customization today's customers require.

BTO manufacturing and virtual factories have also created a surge in outsourcing. Outsourcing is the transfer of a defined "non-core" competency to an identified partner so a company can exploit the partner's expertise while concentrating on its own core competencies. The most renowned form is Contract Electronics Manufacturing (CEM). Ten years ago, no one had heard the term CEM. Today, more electronics manufacturing is outsourced to CEMs than is done internally by the companies for which the CEMs work. Deverticalization is another reality of today. Deverticalization is a form of outsourcing in which the vertical integration that was the focus of conglomerates in prior decades is segmented, resulting in the conglomerates' divesting

WHO IS USING FLOW MANUFACTURING?

————Companies like Trane, VisionTek, and NACCO are using flow manufacturing techniques to maximize product quality and reduce cycle times. For example, Trane's La Crosse Business Unit (LBU) in La Crosse, Wisconsin, has used flow manufacturing to achieve an 18 percent reduction in floor space requirements, turn-around time of 12 days down from 56 days, reduction of working capital from 12 cents per dollar to .004 cents per dollar, and has shortened production time by 33 percent. One of the techniques Trane's LBU used to implement flow manufacturing was to custom-build a system called On-line Automated Shop Information System (OASIS). The system integrates annotated product graphics, process definitions, bills of material, production sequence, quality reporting, and engineering specifications into a graphical representation of each workstation's work elements called "method sheets."

Sherri Everson, the process quality manager for Trane's LBU, says, "Method sheets remind the production operator of the work to be done at the workstation, and when a refresher is needed, the sequence of events is available at the touch of a finger. Changes can be quickly communicated to the shop floor regardless of whether it's a customer change, design change, or process change. We don't need to find and destroy incorrect documentation and can spend more time planning changes and improving processes."

–Manufacturing Systems, April 2000

many of the supply chain links that were not truly core competencies. Software companies have taken note of these developments and created software designed to support BTO, using the Internet to collaborate and communicate.

So, what does all this mean? It means that change is change is change. It means that we live in exhilarating times that demand a new set of rules. It means that the word "company" has a new definition. According to Robert B. Reich in his article "Your Job is Change" (The American Prospect Online, Aug. 21, 2000), it now refers to a "living organism competing, collaborating, and co-creating in a network of other companies."

Therefore, to succeed, a company must take on the role of a "change insurgent," emphasizing organizational readiness rather than specific products or markets. It must seek technologies for business applications, or "killer apps," and look at other organizations with a view to capturing newly emerging technologies and markets at the speed of light. It must be flexible and modular, ready to suddenly change direction. It should source services and supplies through the Web, give suppliers equity, and rely on performance-based pay, stock options, project teams, and contract workers. It should, in short, be a Future Capable Company.

NEW BREED: NEW RULES

Today's company is morphing into a diversified entity, exploring different revenue sources that add value and increase profits. This is changing the rules of competition and shaking up entire industries. Some of these new rules include:

- Using the right mix of old employees, new talent, and technology to generate creative tension, disturb the status quo, and propel the company forward
- Establishing direct links with customers to listen to their needs, complaints, opinions, and suggestions
- Creating alliances between IT (those who create and morph technology) and the salespeople (those who communicate with customers on a regular basis)
- Emphasizing that change is constant and should neither be feared nor resisted, but embraced
- Establishing new measures of success
- Embracing continuous improvement as a prerequisite for success

By following these new rules, the Future Capable Company accepts and understands that boundaries and channels are blurring, thanks to the sweeping changes of the last decade. No longer can manufacturing be contained in a large factory that owns raw materials plants, manufactures parts from those raw materials, assembles them, creates buffer stock from the assemblies, and ships them to the warehouse. No longer can manufacturing exist in a vacuum as one link not fully synthesized in the supply chain.

As discussed in the sections above, today's factory may very well be virtual, with manufacturing functionalities existing in every link in the supply chain. Suppliers, manufacturers, and customers must cooperate and collaborate together to survive in the war of supply chain vs. supply chain. They must practice Supply Chain Synthesis (SCS), which is the holistic, continuous improvement process of ensuring customer satisfaction from the original raw material provider to the ultimate, finished-product consumer. Therefore, a critical portion of the Future Capable Company's organizational readiness is making sure it is ready to achieve SCS.

KEEPING AN EYE ON CHANGE

What would you call a company that has a solid grasp on more than three-quarters of its market, a gross profit margin of 58 percent, and net earnings that have made it the most profitable company of its size in the world? This is a company that has doubled in size roughly every 24 months. What words do you use to describe such a company?

One label that comes to mind is "hyper-aggressive." Another one is "greedy!" If you were feeling kinder, maybe you'd call it "relentlessly opportunistic." Whatever the label, you are describing Intel, the world's largest maker of processor chips for computers and cell phones and handheld devices of all kinds. The captains with their hands on on the helm of the juggernauts and their eyes on change are Chairman Andy Grove and CEO Craig Barrett.

The two understand that the only way to meet challenge is with change, improvement, research, and reinvention.

At a time a few years ago when Intel was faced with greater competition than ever from a new chip

Continued

KEEPING AN EYE ON CHANGE *Continued from page 7*

developed jointly by IBM, Motorola and Apple Computer, how did Intel respond? It poured $1.1 billion on research and development and $2.4 billion on capital investment. At the same time, Intel developed not only the next products, but also the product after the next product, the product after that and the product after that and pursued a whole new market—consumer electronics.

When asked if Intel would be doing what it was doing without a threat poised on the horizon, he responded, "Truthfully, no. We are making gutsier moves investment-wise, pricing-wise—every way, because we've got a competitive threat. The next result is we'll get to advance to the next level of competition."

Barrett sounded the same signal when talking about challenges Intel faced as technology stocks got beaten up in the first half of 2001. Clearly undeterred, Intel is keeping its eye on the next challenge and the next opportunity. It understands the opportunity presented by the change the Internet is bringing around the globe.

"What we really have to do is prepare for the next upswing.... The simple way to be prepared for the upswing is that you never save your way out of a downturn. You never save your way out of a recession. The only way you come out of a recession stronger than when you went into it is by creating great new technology, great new products," Barrett said. "We'll focus on the Internet and how vibrant the Internet is, what an early stage of the Internet build-out we have, which is why we should all be excited about the opportunity we have."

Barrett added, "The world is going digital. And whether it's communication, whether it's access to information, whether it's conducting commerce, we're all going digital. And this digital world is what is exciting and what is the opportunity for us all.... The real hotbed of activity in Internet commerce is and continues to be, and will be for the foreseeable future, business-to-business commerce. That's where you're getting complete renovation of the supply chain analysis, business-to-consumer, business-to-supplier, and business-to-customer type of activities."

Now that is leadership that keeps its eyes on change and sees all that it can see. That is leadership at a Future Capable Company.

In the following chapter, I discuss the changing nature of business-to-business and business-to-consumer relationships and how manufacturing is being affected by these relationships. In the remaining chapters, I tell you what being a Future Capable Company means, introduce the 12 Future Capable Company Requirements of Success, discuss how to achieve each of the 12 requirements, and identify the Future Capable Company Path Forward.

Transforming your company into a Future Capable Company requires patience, hard work, and perseverance. Your organization cannot become a Future Capable Company overnight. However, if you apply the knowledge you will gain from this book, your transformation will be both smooth and successful.

chapter 2

Manufacturing and the Internet

ot too long ago, business-to-business (B2B) was the hot topic. In 1999 and much of 2000, you couldn't pick up the newspaper or a magazine, watch television, or log on to your favorite Website without seeing an announcement that yet another company or group of companies was moving its B2B transactions to the Web. Companies believed it would cut costs, reinvent supply chains, improve communications, and improve customer satisfaction. Thus, almost overnight, they were trying to transition into this new business model in anticipation of gaining new market share, conquering material cost inflation, and increasing profit margins.

In recent months, however, we've read and heard a lot about how most dot-coms (B2B and B2C) have become dot-bombs. According to Boston Consulting Group, from September 1999 to October 2000, more than 100 dot-coms failed. Some went bankrupt, others made huge cuts in their work force, and others drastically re-wrote their business plans. Most of them simply shut down their Websites ("What detonated the dot-bombs?" USA Today, December 4, 2000.) Industry experts blame the failures on everything from emphasis on revenues, not profits, to interest rate hikes in 2000.

The assumption here is that, because so many dot-coms are now dot-bombs, e- is dead. Companies that had grandiose plans for creating B2B cyber marketplaces, extranets, and trading portals have either scaled back their plans or put them on hold indefinitely. The attitude is, "Well, we tried e-, but it didn't work. Now, it's back to the old ways of doing business." In other words, B2B has become Back 2 Basics.

My answer to that is simple. All assumptions are wrong. We should not throw the baby out with the bathwater. These doomsday prophets are looking down a mineshaft, unable to see the peak of the mountain above, let alone the next peak. The Internet is still the most important invention of the last 100 years. It has irrevocably changed the way we do business, the way our customers shop, and the way we manufacture products. It has and will continue to totally reinvent business in ways we cannot imagine. Therefore, the idea of B2B is not what went wrong, but how it was pursued. We did not do the correct things to make it a success.

Despite all the hoopla, few companies have a consistent definition of B2B and B2C. Without a consistent definition, it is difficult to see where B2C and B2B fit into a company's current business model or decide which technology can support it. Yet, to be a Future Capable Company, an organization must be able to integrate B2B and B2C, for only then will it be ready to achieve SCS. Most importantly, the Future Capable Company must practice an expanded form of B2B and B2C, one I call B2B2B2B2B2C. This chapter discusses the various forms of B2B and B2C, defines B2B2B2B2B2C, and discusses why it will yield a victory in the war of supply chains.

UNDERSTANDING B2B

There is no one definitive form of B2B. In reality, there are three broad categories of B2B, as shown in Figure 1.

The simplest form of B2B is Model A in the illustration. It involves direct one-to-one communications between two organizations, an approach I refer to as Internet EDI. Functionally, it is basically an upgrade of the EDI initiatives put in place in the past 20 years. Universal protocols are used to share data so that organizations with different computer platforms can communicate electronically.

From a supply chain perspective, Model A accommodates supply chain link optimization. However, it does not position an organization to benefit from the advantages of a synthesized supply chain. It is most appropriately used in proprietary relationships.

The second form is Model B. It is a simple many-to-many business model, and the fastest-growing form of B2B. Using the almost unlimited capacities of the World Wide Web, companies create marketplaces where they can access and share data with numerous organizations at one time. An example is the maintenance, repairs, and operations (MRO) marketplace. There, an organization can poll a wide range of providers to find the availability and price of a needed part in a single transaction. Suppliers can process the request with automated front-end processors and respond to the inquiry in seconds. Such marketplaces now exist in more than 25 industries, including steel, plastics, auto parts, fasteners, and even cattle.

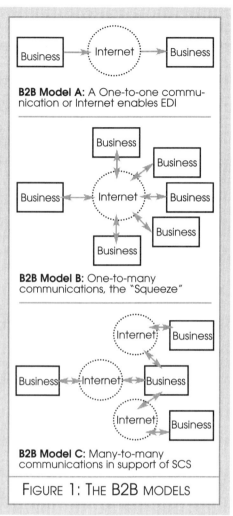

B2B Model A: A One-to-one communication or Internet enables EDI

B2B Model B: One-to-many communications, the "Squeeze"

B2B Model C: Many-to-many communications in support of SCS

FIGURE 1: THE B2B MODELS

Unfortunately, major companies are not using these marketplaces to synthesize the supply chain, share production information, or promote collaboration. Rather, they view them as a mechanism for squeezing suppliers for the best possible price through a "reverse bid" process: A company will post an order for a product along with the last price paid for that item, inviting suppliers to openly bid for the order by under-pricing one another. This practice is under investigation by the Federal Trade Commission as being in violation of antitrust laws and as a form of collusion and price fixing. More

MRO MARKETPLACE: MANUFACTURING.NET LLC

Cahners Business Information and Aspect Development Inc. formed a new company called Manufacturing.Net LLC to provide the manufacturing industry with an electronic marketplace. The new company is built around www.manufacturing.net, a Website Cahners launched in 1996 to provide online content and communities to the manufacturing sector. As a result of the joint venture, e-commerce applications, search technology, and product databases are being added to the site.

Specifically, the site will combine content from 23 Cahners manufacturing publications with an electronic catalog of maintenance, repairs, and operations (MRO) products and services. The catalog contains more than 1.8 million total products, services, and suppliers throughout the entire manufacturing supply chain, from planning and purchasing to shipping and delivery. Customers will be able to make secure, real-time transactions through the site.

"We're revolutionizing the way MRO purchasing is done," says Cahners CEO Marc Teren. "We are the first to combine a complete e-business capability with a wealth of information for manufacturing professionals in an easily accessible format, including up-to-date product information, economic statistics and industry-specific news and research."

The Manufacturing.Net Website gets more than 1 million hits monthly, has more than 220,000 registered users, and has more than 360 advertisers. In addition, more than 77,000 subscribers receive a customized weekly newsletter with proprietary content.

importantly, it is not cost-effective in the long run.

The third form of B2B is an advanced business practice that utilizes the entire supply chain and the Web to satisfy the customer. I call this B2B2B2B2B. B2B2B2B2B allows an organization to share use or procurement data directly and simultaneously all along the supply chain. Each organization can react to the information, allowing for a smooth flow of material through the supply chain. This model provides visibility to each organization in the supply chain, and each can take independent action or a group can take collective action as needed.

An example is a project we did for a group of manufacturers. These manufacturers supplied products to more than 2,000 businesses, and they made separate shipments to all these businesses. This was costly and time-consuming. Tompkins used B2B2B2B2B to create a single point from which these 2,000 businesses could order and created a single pull center from which the manufacturers could ship. This converted less-than-truckloads (LTLs) shipments to full truckloads. It also created a single invoice, decreased the cost of administration, and created huge inventory savings.

B2B2B2B2B is the only form of B2B that will yield the desired results. It is important to understand this and focus on it. If your organization doesn't understand this and tries to get by with Model A or Model B or both, it will not be a Future Capable Company.

THE B2C CONNECTION: B2B2B2B2B2C

Business-to-consumer (B2C) is often perceived as distinctly separate from the B2B business models. In actuality, when B2C is treated as a form of direct-to-consumer sales, it is a variant of the "A" and "B" models previously outlined. The consumer transaction triggers the rest of the supply chain. Like the MRO marketplace business customer, the consumer can search for and research a number of product sources, selecting the one offering the best value of price and service. At the supplier's end, the sales transaction results in an order that is relayed throughout the supply chain, resulting in a movement of material forward to fulfill the customer's needs.

In reality, just like B2B, B2C takes more than one form. Yes, it can be a direct-to-consumer online transaction. However, on a larger scale, it is also the desired result of all B2B sales and transactions along the supply chain. Consider an automobile manufacturer, for example. The manufacturer does not order parts on a whim; the manufacturer is in the business of building automobiles for its customers, and it needs those parts for that reason. Thus, B2B2B2B2B becomes B2B2B2B2B2C—a holistic, continuous improvement process of ensuring customer satisfaction from the original raw material

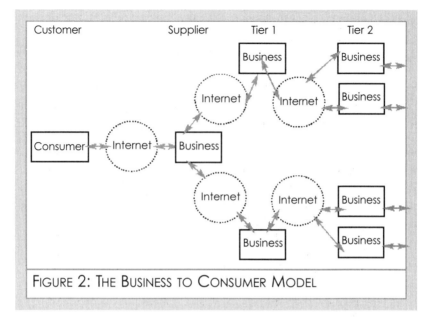

FIGURE 2: THE BUSINESS TO CONSUMER MODEL

provider to the ultimate finished-product consumer.

Does that definition seem familiar? It should, because it is the definition of SCS. SCS is the synthesis of the supply chain where synthesis is the integration and the unification of supply chain links to form a whole. SCS has No Boundaries. It also recognizes that competition in today's marketplace is not company vs. company, but supply chain vs. supply chain and that sometimes companies that were once like fighting siblings are now allies in the war between supply chains. So, in actuality B2B2B2B2B2C is just another acronym for SCS.

THE FUTURE CAPABLE COMPANY AND B2B2B2B2B2C/SCS

A Future Capable Company must have a sound B2B2B2B2B2C/SCS strategy. Such a strategy requires a clear understanding of what the customer perceives as value. Often this can mean the product with the best quality offered at the lowest cost and with the tightest possible lead-times. It must then deliver that value, focusing on core competencies while removing excess, duplication, and waste.

As I noted earlier, many of the B2B strategies being promoted in today's Web-based environment focus solely on a single link in the chain, limiting the ability of the organizations to benefit from one another. The inherent limitations and inefficiencies of a link relationship prevent the supply chain from competing in the marketplace. Success is based on the overall performance of the supply chain. The B2B strategy that encompasses the practices and philosophy of SCS is the B2B2B2B2B2C model.

The foundation of SCS is a collective focus of members of the supply chain on the customer. Increased value and customer satisfaction become the responsibility of every member of the chain, not just the link closest to the consumer. The result? Members of the chain function as a united organization that practices continuous improvement to win the customer and benefits from each win.

How do these organizations do this? How is SCS achieved? To achieve SCS, an organization must first understand and practice eight core competencies: Change, Peak-to-Peak Performance, Total Operations, Customer Satisfaction, Manufacturing Synthesis, Distribution Synthesis, Partnerships, and Communications.

Understanding Change means understanding that no person or

INTERNET-BASED SUPPLY CHAIN: PETSMART

Petsmart International Supply Company has adopted an Internet-based procurement solution. As a result, the company has seen travel costs fall by 60 percent; phone and fax costs are also lower.

This procurement system requires suppliers to present their goods in a standardized way, including digital photographs. Structured buying and information processes have saved the company time and money, while reducing inventory by 20 percent.

Product choice has increased 40 percent while time-to-market has become 50 percent faster. Marcia Meyer, the president of Petsmart, says that electronic procurement has been beneficial for everyone involved. "Everyone is making more money and earnings on this."

–ebiz, August 3, 2000

organization can manage Change. Instead, a person or organization must harness the energy of Change. The supply chain is not in a steady state. Harnessing change means adopting a continuous improvement process that permanently rekindles individual creativity and responsibility and creates a transformation of a company's internal and external relationships—relationships with No Boundaries.

Peak-to-Peak Performance involves the continuous process of beginning anew and climbing to a new peak, and then the next peak, and then the peak after that. In other words, a company should not wait for outside factors to force its hand, but instead be innovative on its own terms and prepare for challenges before they arise, while being wary of the naysayers. Peak-to-Peak Performance requires innovation and preparation for challenges before they arise.

Total Operations is the integration of the warehouse, logistics, manufacturing, quality, maintenance, organizational excellence, and systems. Like SCS, it is a holistic process, and it stretches from the planning of a site through the determination of the correct network to the cultural ties that bind employees to an organization's mission. It is based on collaboration both inside and outside the organization, relying on teams that focus on ongoing incremental improvements, as well as innovation, communication, and leadership.

Customer Satisfaction is the means by which companies attempt to differentiate their products, keep customers loyal, improve profits, and become the suppliers of choice. Customer Satisfaction must not be confused with customer service, which measures company performance against an internally generated requirement. Customer Satisfaction is a scientific process that requires companies to divest themselves of their self-interests while fixating on the needs, expectations, and perceptions of those to whom they provide products and services.

As SKU customization and customer-ready product preparation become postponed to the last possible moment, traditional roles in manufacturing are becoming less of a means for securing competitive advantage. To remove the boundaries from manufacturing and merge these traditional roles, Manufacturing Synthesis is necessary. Manufacturing Synthesis combines Lean Manufacturing, agile Manufacturing, and Winning Manufacturing, and it incorporates cellular Manufacturing.

Distribution Synthesis is making sure that the right manufacturing operations and right distribution centers are in the right locations and hold the right amount of inventory, and that the right transportation is being used to fulfill the order to the satisfaction of the customer. The results are reduced inventory investments, reduced distribution costs, improved customer satisfaction, and a streamlined flow of goods to the marketplace. It requires blurring the boundaries between warehousing and transportation, using a hybrid push/pull system that adjusts to more demanding customer-satisfaction requirements.

True Partnerships are long-term collaborative relationships. They are based on trust and a mutual desire to work together for the benefit of the other partner and the Partnership. Forming a true Partnership means discarding the traditional relationships that are commonly found between organizations today.

SCS Communication is simultaneous, instantaneous, and multidirectional to allow all supply chain partners to work at the same time rather than sequentially. This eliminates inventory buffers and accelerates cash flow. It also allows dynamic planning, which replaces the outdated practice of long-term forecasting. Strategic information is available to all partners so that all have contact with the customer and are aware of changing needs and trends. SCS Communication, then, is B2B2B2B2B.

An excellent example of SCS Communication is Collaborative Planning, Forecasting, and Replenishment (CPFR). CPFR allows collaborative processes across the supply chain, using a set of processes and technologies that are open, flexible, extensible, and support a broad set of requirements, including new data types and interoperability. CPFR also allows customers to contribute to the generation of numbers and participate in other parts of the process. It changes relationships from buyer/seller to partner/partner as customer and purchase orders become collaborative forecast and replenishment orders.

CPFR uses Internet technologies like XML, which structures and defines data for easy integration between systems, and the World Wide Web to promote the real-time, global, secure, and simultaneous communications that are its hallmark. Secure communication is critical for establishing trust between supply chain partners. Simultaneous communication is vital to the CPFR process because information must be shared between all interested parties at the same time. Otherwise, the supply chain remains time-phased and linear, rather than nimble and responsive.

Once each organization masters and practices these eight SCS core competencies, they have the tools for the second part of SCS, which incorporates supply chain design, supply chain planning, and supply chain execution.

Supply chain design means designing for SCS. It is the first step in the process and is design at the highest level. It comprises network design, inventory design, transportation design, and customer satisfaction design.

Supply chain planning follows supply chain design. It is a detailed planning process that is created to meet the needs identified in the supply chain design process. Supply chain planning involves demand planning, event planning, inventory planning, replenishment planning, manufacturing planning, and transportation planning.

Supply chain execution is the final part of the process of achieving SCS. Supply chain execution involves the systems that address SCS in real time: order management, warehouse management, transportation management, and manufacturing management. The Internet plays a role in the process as well—it is the means by which communication between supply chain planning and supply chain execution are accomplished. This second part of SCS is discussed at greater length in Chapter 15.

The technology and approach of the B2B2B2B2B model complement and enhance the functional aspects of B2B2B2B2B2C/SCS, providing the vital mechanism for distributing critical data across the supply chain. The visibility of materials used is also shared across the chain in near real time, allowing for advanced planning and scheduling, reducing total WIP, shortening lead-times, and delivering optimum value and service to the end consumer. These objectives are the objectives of the Future Capable Company, so it is evident that the Future Capable Company must embrace and practice B2B2B2B2B2C/SCS.

chapter 3

The Future Capable Company and 12 Requirements of Success

 s I stated in Chapter 2, as product customization and customer-ready product preparation become postponed until the last possible minute, traditional roles in manufacturing become less of a means of securing competitive advantage. How can a manufacturing organization secure this advantage if everything that has allowed it to compete in years past is no longer viable? By becoming a Future Capable Company.

A Future Capable Company is on a never-ending journey of continuous improvement. It produces quality products, satisfies customers, identifies manufacturing as a strategic strength and an important link in the synthesized supply chain, increases its return on assets, and reduces costs. A Future Capable Company is totally prepared for B2B2B2B2B2C/SCS. Not only does it focus on the best solution for today's requirements, it goes beyond that solution and focuses on the solution after next.

Becoming a Future Capable Company requires a consistent direction, shared by the entire organization. Manufacturing managers, conferences, speeches, and books often get sidetracked on macroeconomic issues that, although interesting, are inconsistent with this shared consistent direction and are, therefore, irrelevant to your path forward. Discussions of these macroeconomic issues often include:

- An analysis of the service sector vs. the manufacturing sector of the economy. The results of this analysis range from the opinion that the service sector is supreme to the conclusion that the manufacturing sector is the driver of a nation's standard of living.
- An analysis of the manufacturing productivity of various nations. The results here vary from the United States' being last in the productivity race to the United States' being first in the same race.
- An analysis of the cost of labor from one nation to another. Once again, the conclusions reached on this point vary from one extreme to the other.
- The impact of budget deficits, the valuation of the dollar, tax laws, trade policies, government regulations, and more. The number of opinions on these topics and the effect of these issues seem to be limited only by the number of authors in print. Certainly, no matter what you believe, there is at least one author who presents an acceptable position.

Similarly, it is easy to get sidetracked by dwelling on poor management issues, such as:

- Short-term orientation and results measurement
- Improper return on investment and accounting procedures to justify capital expenditures
- An orientation toward acquiring business instead of building business
- Poor implementation of technology
- Ineffective methods for dealing with unions
- Poor development of managers

Although both sets of issues are important in their own ways they are not on the Future Capable Company's agenda. Rather, they can bog down a company and create blinders that prevent growth and continuous improvement. A Future Capable Company goes beyond them to look at the important issues. These issues are:

- All great nations will have great manufacturing capabilities.
- The United States is the overall leader in manufacturing productivity.
- A discussion of direct labor costs from nation to nation is irrelevant.
- You cannot be successful without embracing the new economy.
- Business no longer ends at the border of a particular country or continent.
- All assumptions are wrong.
- You cannot predict the future based on the past.

With these big-picture issues in mind, the Future Capable Company gets on with its operations, responding to the forces of Change and Integration while using the proper application of technology. It harnesses the power of Change while integrating all operations and applying the economically justifiable technology for today's and tomorrow's requirements. This chapter discusses Responding to Change, Integration and the Future Capable Company, and Technology for the Future Capable Company. It then outlines the 12 Requirements of Success for the Future Capable Company.

RESPONDING TO CHANGE

To respond to Change, the Future Capable Company must be:
- Flexible—able to handle a variety of requirements without being altered. This means using manufacturing systems that are "soft" and "friendly," rather than "hard" or "rigid." They are able to address changes in variety and handle products that vary in size and features.
- Modular—accommodating fluctuations in volume. Modular manufacturing operations can produce more or less of a product without changing the method. Systems operate efficiently over a wide range of operating rates.
- Upgradeable—gracefully incorporating advances in equipment systems and technology so that operations are able to move to the next level without stumbling or hiccupping and with little downtime.
- Adaptable—taking into consideration the implications of calendars, seasons, and peaks and recognizing that product demand varies greatly over time and the ability to adjust accordingly.
- Selectively operable—operating in segments, allowing for implementation of one segment at a time without degradation of the manufacturing process. Selective operability requires understanding how

each segment operates, and it allows contingency plans to be put in place.

- Automation supportive—supporting the implementation of automation throughout the company and beyond, as well as being able to integrate and interface with all automated elements.

These qualities allow the Future Capable Company to pursue a process of continuous improvement to address the ongoing, never-ending pace of Change.

INTEGRATION AND THE FUTURE CAPABLE COMPANY

The elements that the Future Capable Company must understand to achieve Integration are:

- Total Integration—the integration of material and information flow in a true, top-down progression that begins with the customer.
- Blurred boundaries—the elimination of the traditional customer/supplier and manufacturing/warehousing relationships, as well as those between order entry, service, manufacturing, and distribution.
- Consolidation—the merging of similar and disparate business entities that results in fewer and stronger competitors, customers, and suppliers. Consolidation also includes the physical merging of sites, companies, and functions.
- Reliability—the implementation of robust systems, redundant systems, and fault-tolerant systems to create very high levels of uptime.
- Maintenance—a combination of preventive and predictive maintenance. Preventive maintenance is a continuous process that minimizes future maintenance problems. Predictive maintenance anticipates potential problems by sensing the operations of a machine or system. This is discussed in more detail in Chapter 12.
- Economic progressiveness—the adoption of innovative fiscal practices that integrate dispersed information into a whole that may be used for decision making.

These elements create a broad, holistic perspective of Integration that must be embraced to become a Future Capable Company.

TECHNOLOGY AND THE FUTURE CAPABLE COMPANY

Communication systems and networks, particularly the Internet, are being used to create new partnerships and alliances almost daily. Actually, there has been so much excitement about the promise of technology and how it can link suppliers, retailers, and customers that an important point has been lost: The specific systems used to perform the links are not important. What is important is that technology be used to create simultaneous, instantaneous, and multidirectional internal and external communications to allow real-time work and not sequential work.

The Future Capable Company realizes that IT used in this manner can eliminate inventory buffers and accelerate the flow of cash. A Future Capable Company's IT system, therefore, integrates three kinds of capabilities:

• Day-to-day and Internet transactions and communications that align supply and demand by sharing orders and daily schedules

• Planning and decision making that support the demand and shipment planning necessary for distributing resources effectively

• An integrated network model that supports continuous improvement

In other words, the Future Capable Company's technology facilitates dynamic planning, which replaces the outdated practice of long-term forecasting and allows all involved to respond to changing needs and trends.

DYNAMIC CONSISTENCY

Responding to Change, achieving integration, and applying technology successfully requires dynamic consistency. To understand dynamic consistency, let's step back and look at a bigger picture. In industry today, there are three basic types of organizations:

Type I Organizations: Static Consistency

Type II Organizations: Dynamic Inconsistency

Type III Organizations: Dynamic Consistency

Type I organizations resist change. They pride themselves on maintaining the status quo and seldom realize there is an opportunity to improve. Type I managers believe:

- "We have optimized our operations, and there is no room for improvement."
- "We have always been profitable, why should we change anything?"

Type I organizations, therefore, are not Future Capable Companies.

Type II organizations are dynamic, inconsistent organizations. They realize they are not successful and are actively installing new programs. They are busy organizations. Everyone is on a task force or two, but no one has a chance to work as the entire day is spent in meetings. There is no shared direction of where they are headed. Each person has his or her own direction. Although there are islands of success, the company as a whole is not improving. Managers within Type II organizations are frustrated; the harder they work, the more they seem to lose. Although they are not Future Capable Companies, Type II organizations are actively pursuing manufacturing improvements and would benefit most from the process of becoming a Future Capable Company.

Type III organizations truly understand the meaning of dynamic consistency. They are driven by an "improve, improve, improve" mentality based upon a consistent direction of manufacturing. Such dynamic, consistent organizations are Future Capable Companies.

An example of a Future Capable Company is Cisco Systems, which uses a combination of Lean manufacturing, outsourcing, alliances, and Internet technology to dominate its market share. Cisco's CEO, John Chambers, believes that to survive, a company must constantly reinvent itself, and that's why he stresses customer focus and continuous improvement. This is dynamic consistency at its best.

CISCO SYSTEMS: A FUTURE CAPABLE COMPANY

In 1984, Sandra Lerner and Len Bosack, two Stanford University employees, founded Cisco Systems to create devices that can "route" data traffic from one computer network to another, a difficult proposition at that time

CISCO SYSTEMS

because most computers could not communicate with one another. In the 15 years that followed, the company has doubled in size every year and now has 29,000 employees, revenues of $12 billion, and profits of $3 billion over the past four quarters.

Although routers are still Cisco's main business (it supplies about 80 percent of the Internet's routers), the company has diversified into other networking hardware-from switches for telephone networks to devices that link homes to the Internet, and from equipment for high-speed optical fiber to wireless communications. Much of this hardware depends on Cisco's software. Its engineers develop programs that run on all this networking equipment like the Internet-working Operating System (IOS) that lets, for example, Cisco routers talk to one another and can manage corporate data networks. Cisco also adds new technology by buying start-ups: since 1993, it has acquired 55 firms at a total cost of more than $24 billion. Last August, for example, it bought Cerent, a telecommunications equipment maker that manufactures switches for high-speed optical networks.

Cisco is also a virtual manufacturer. The company operates only a few factories for assembling its most sophisticated products. The rest of its equipment is built in three dozen plants around the world run by contract manufacturers. Data connections that send test software, design files, and order information allow these manufacturers to produce to Cisco's specifications.

Much of Cisco's success hinges on the fact that it sells critical global communications equipment. However, it is more likely that it will meet CEO John Chambers' goals to generate revenues of $50 billion by 2004 and to become the first company worth $1 trillion because it is constantly reinventing itself. Chambers is a firm believer in customer focus and continuous improvement. His focus on continuous improvement is evident when, at the end of each speech, he asks his audience what he could have done better. His dedication to the customer is exemplified by the story that he was late for his first board meeting as chief executive because a customer needed help.

–The Economist, April 6, 2000

THE 12 REQUIREMENTS OF SUCCESS FOR THE FUTURE CAPABLE COMPANY

Dynamic consistency means having a consistent company direction. At Dow Jones, this is referred to as the "bedrocks." At Toyota, it is "the philosophies of business." The Future Capable Company has "12 Requirements of Success":

1. Cost. Scrutinizing transportation, acquisition, distribution, inventory, reverse logistics, packaging, and manufacturing and examining the supply chain for ways to significantly reduce costs and increase profitability. The Future Capable Company recognizes that cost reduction within the plant is of value only if those lower costs are passed along the entire supply chain.

2. Customer Satisfaction is an ongoing, escalating process of meeting customer requirements and exceeding customer expectations. Future Capable Companies are responsive to customer needs through customization. They understand value-added activities, and are flexible, modular, and adaptable. The Future Capable Company strives for high quality while maintaining high value.

3. Global. Business no longer has borders. The Future Capable Company must realize that success depends heavily on an integrated global strategy. To reach its full market potential, the Future Capable Company must reach out to other countries and push aside boundaries to promulgate its goods and services. If you are not everywhere, you are nowhere.

4. Speed. Today's business climate may be described in the words of three-time, national, off-road motorcycling champion Chris Stewart: "If you go slow, you will fall." Future Capable Companies must be able to "ride fast," to use BTO, to respond to the customer, and to be quick. As John Chambers of Cisco Systems says, "It's not the big that beat the small, but the fast that beat the slow."

5. Certainty/Change. A Future Capable Company must manage certainty by establishing, accepting, and following standards of performance. When activities conform to well-established and clear standards, errors, disruptions, and crises are rare. Change must be expected, harnessed, and responded to smoothly, however.

6. Control. A Future Capable Company must practice control with a

straightforward and transparent inventory control system, efficient material flow, and up-to-date and upgradable material tracking and control while simplifying all processes.

7. Balance. Future Capable Companies must have balanced manufacturing and supply chain operations that result in drastic inventory reductions. They have no need for large inventories and will achieve balance throughout the supply chain while exceeding customer expectations.

8. Quality. The Future Capable Company must reject the various quality crusades and the quality hype of the last several decades and work to understand that quality is conformance to customer requirements. It must then put a continuous quality improvement process in place.

9. Maintenance. The Future Capable Company must fully understand the scope of the maintenance management process because maintenance is much more than just the care of physical assets used in a production operation. Maintenance for the Future Capable Company combines reliability, predictive maintenance, and preventive maintenance to create high levels of uptime and productivity, anticipate potential problems, and minimize future problems. Maintenance and operations must be integrated and function as a supportive team through improved planning, scheduling, and cooperative, team-based improvement efforts.

10. Human Capital. Future Capable Companies must view employees as their most important assets because without this commitment, continuous improvement will not be achieved. Organizations must value intellectual capital and secure its growth by making sure all employees are satisfied, happy, and challenged.

11. Continuous Improvement. With the pace of Change and the rate of innovation, what is a great process today will be suspect in a few months and obsolete shortly thereafter. The Future Capable Company must be aware of this and continually evaluate, analyze, and improve processes.

12. Synthesis. The Future Capable Company must synthesize all functions. It must strive to achieve Supply Chain Synthesis by making sure that decisions are made in the context of the supply chain and the needs of the ultimate customer.

The 12 Requirements of Success for the Future Capable Company are the foundation for this book. Meeting these requirements takes time, patience, energy, perseverance, and, most importantly, quality leadership.

LEAD ON

No company can meet the 12 Requirements of Success without leaders to hold up the vision of the Future Capable Company, remind people of its benefits, set the Future Capable Company path forward, and reward faithfulness and courage. Future Capable Company leaders should exhibit energy, intensity, passion, and determination to continuously aspire to their vision of the Future Capable Company.

Leaders who can create a Future Capable Company must have:
• Integrity—they must live and tell the truth.
• Credibility—they must be accountable, genuine, and open.
• Enthusiasm—they must show their excitement about the future.
• Optimism—they must focus on success.
• Urgency—they must know that the only way to impact the future is to act today.
• Determination—they must step forward in the face of doubts and uncertainties to accept risk and move forward. In other words, they act.

Relying on these characteristics, the Future Capable Company leaders must motivate by the way they communicate, work, and treat others. They must recognize the importance of effective communication and arm others with the certainty and control that allows them to harness the energy of Change. When these leaders make decisions, they must adhere to the three rights: the right decisions at the right time communicated to the right people.

Those who lead a Future Capable Company must also be able to revolutionize their organizations. This means going beyond simple cultural changes and perceptions and transforming the rules, habits, procedures, standards, norms, rewards, language, jargon, stories, expectations, ceremonies, and titles that affect cultural conformance, organizational behavior, and organizational performance. The foundation for this must be the shared, consistent direction discussed earlier in this chapter. The leaders must be responsible for aligning everyone with a commitment to dynamic consistency and to the ultimate customer.

The 12 Requirements of Success for the Future Capable Company are not quick fixes; they must become the company's heartbeat. That is why quality leaders are so important. If you are ready for this way of life and you have the committed, quality leadership necessary for becoming a Future Capable Company, then you can get started. A good place to start is with the first of the 12 Requirements of Success: Cost. Chapter 4 shows you how. Chapters 5-15 then show you how you can achieve the rest.

chapter 4
COST

Future Capable Company must scrutinize transportation costs, acquisition costs, distribution costs, inventory carrying costs, reverse logistics costs, packaging costs, and manufacturing costs and look all along the supply chain for ways to reduce them significantly and increase profitability.

The Future Capable Company is aware that reducing costs and then further reducing costs is critical to success. Its methods of cost reduction differ from those of the Type I and Type II organizations, just as its methods of responding to change differ from theirs. This chapter takes a brief look at how Type I and Type II organizations reduce costs, then examines Future Capable Company cost reductions in more detail.

TYPE I ORGANIZATION COST REDUCTIONS

Type I organizations set a goal of reducing costs by a couple of percentage points per year. This approach results in a wide variety of limited-scope, cost-cutting measures. Examples include:

- Consolidation of forms to eliminate excess paperwork
- Re-layout of workstations to minimize operator walking
- Redesign of shipping cartons to reduce the cost of packaging and materials
- Installation of load detectors on conveyors to save energy
- Recycling scrap material

These measures are more focused on containing costs than reducing them. They are also departmental cost-cutting measures that are often implemented at the expense of other departments. Often, they also are implemented without full explanation or training on new methods. This sort of cost-cutting siloism rarely benefits anyone, not even the departments that implement it. Often, the cost reductions are short-term and do little to minimize costs in the long run.

For example, we worked with a company that, when we started, was a Type III organization. They wanted us to help them implement Type III organization cost-cutting processes. They were interested in dynamic consistency, long-term cost-reduction processes, and business process continuous improvement (BPCI), a leadership-driven process of collaboration that uses teams and a shared Model of Success to change company culture and operating style. Major success occurred. However, as a result of the sale of the company, a new management team was put in place whose focus was on Type I cost-cutting measures. Siloism became rampant in the organization, as did resistance to any kind of change. In the end, number crunching was the only emphasis. The result? A Type III organization became a Type I organization, and no further cost savings resulted from this change.

TYPE II ORGANIZATION COST-CUTTING MEASURES

The cost-cutting measures of Type II organizations are based on link optimization. They set a goal of improving or eliminating one particular factor or process to reduce costs. For example, a Type II organization may decide to reduce inventory-carrying costs, a worthy ideal. However, it will look at only inventory costs without considering other costs. Cost reductions within a link are of value only if they reduce costs within the supply chain.

Type II organizations do not attempt to reduce costs all along the supply chain, which may mean implementing a measure that may not reduce costs in the short-term, but will benefit the supply chain in the long-term. For example, one Type II organization decided to reduce transportation costs by finding a carrier with lower rates. The organization accepted bids and chose a new carrier that was less expensive. However, the organization was so focused on the costs that it did not research the new carrier's delivery times. It turns out that they were longer. Those longer delivery times increased supply chain inventory and therefore did not benefit the organization, its supply chain, or, ultimately, its customers. True cost reduction reduces the supply chain's costs, not just the cost in one link.

FUTURE CAPABLE COMPANY COST REDUCTION

The Future Capable Company believes in continuous cost reductions that are consistent with the overall direction of the company and the supply chain. It scrutinizes transportation costs, acquisition costs, distribution costs, inventory carrying costs, reverse logistics costs, packaging costs, and other costs with an "improve, improve, improve" mindset. Future Capable Companies reduce costs on a day-by-day, step-by-step, dynamic, never-ending basis. They realize that what may be a great way to lower costs today might be only a good way next week, an average way next month, and a poor way next quarter.

A Future Capable Company's cost-reduction measures are for the long-term. What may seem like a cost increase in the short-term may well reduce costs over a longer period. For example, National Linen Service, an Atlanta-based institutional linen services provider, invested in new technology to help it route its private fleet more efficiently. Corporate logistics teams in various regions examined the company's delivery operations using software that maximized routing efficiency. They determined that by redesigning many of their trucks' cargo areas to increase cubic capacity, the fleet could satisfy more customers with fewer vehicles. The combination of software and vehicle redesign reduced the company's fleet by 15 percent and its fleet capital budget by 50 percent without compromising customer satisfaction. In other words, the company spent money in one area to greatly reduce costs in another.

A Future Capable Company's cost reductions come from practicing SCS. With a total supply chain view, the Future Capable Company will make the cost reductions required for supply chain success.

FUTURE CAPABLE COMPANY COST REDUCTION: CANNONDALE

Mountain bikers want bikes that are both light (for riding up steep hills) and stiff (for very fast downhill rides). In 1998, Cannondale designed the Raven, a full-suspension mountain bike with a frame constructed from a lightweight aluminum spine with carbon-reinforced epoxy skins. In an attempt to continue trying to improve customer satisfaction, the Connecticut-based bicycle manufacturer introduced a new design for the Raven in January 2000 that features a lighter, stiffer frame that has delighted mountain bikers and reduced costs at the same time.

The new bike's frame has a lighter magnesium metal spine for absorbing vertical loads and composite skins and a thinner carbon-reinforced nylon composite. Together, the more advanced materials contributed to a half-pound weight reduction for a total weight of 2.5 pounds for the spine and skin. Add all the frame-related hardware and the revamped frame weight comes to just 5.3 pounds—1.3 pounds less than the original frame and roughly twice the weight savings. The nylon composite provides the same stiffness as the thermoset composite of 1998, but it has a new wall geometry that features internal concave recesses and averages 0.010 inches thinner.

The new frame also enabled a cost reduction, which Cannondale estimates at roughly 20 percent. This savings comes from material saved by thinning the skin walls and from increased manufacturing throughput. "The thermoset frame had to cool for an hour," Tod Patterson, a design engineer who worked on the new Raven, explains. "The thermoplastic part only has to cool for a few minutes." This cost reduction even offsets the extra manufacturing steps—a primer and a nylon-based powder coating—needed to protect the magnesium spine from corrosion.

–Design News, January 17, 2000

THE MAGNITUDE OF SIGNIFICANT COST REDUCTIONS

The Cost Requirement of Success states that a Future Capable Company must scrutinize transportation costs, acquisition costs, distribution costs, inventory carrying costs, reverse logistics costs, packaging costs, and manufacturing costs, and look all along the supply chain for ways to reduce them significantly and increase profitability. Cost reductions of two percent, five percent, or even 10 percent are not significant. Significant cost reductions may start at about 20 percent, but ideally, they should range from 40 percent to 60 percent.

The attitude and approach of someone attempting to reduce costs by five percent is totally different from the attitude and approach of someone attempting a 50 percent cost reduction. Five percent reductions are the result of something simple, such as installing software that reduces paperwork; 50 percent reductions require dynamic consistency and include eliminating waste and redundancy while practicing continuous improvement throughout the supply chain. This takes innovation, perseverance, and the ability to see the solution after next. It can mean closing plants, reducing and eliminating inventory, outsourcing functions, and eliminating jobs.

INCREASING PROFITABILITY THROUGH COST REDUCTION: OSHKOSH TRUCKS

Making big trucks can be very profitable. In fact, Oshkosh Truck (Oshkosh, Wisconsin) was recently named to Fortune magazine's "100 Fastest-Growing Companies" list. To be considered for that honor, companies have to demonstrate a 30 percent annual growth rate in both revenue and earnings per share during a three-year period. Last year, Oshkosh Truck sales grew 29 percent, and the 83-year-old company posted record earnings. For the first quarter of fiscal 2000, the company's net income was up 56 percent. To meet growing demand for its products and

Continued

INCREASING PROFITABILITY *Continued from page 37*

reduce manufacturing costs, Oshkosh Truck redesigned its assembly procedures several years ago. The company streamlined its manufacturing process by developing a flexible assembly line at its 215,000 square-foot plant. That flexible production means Oshkosh workers can assemble both military and civilian vehicles simultaneously.

In the past, Oshkosh Truck used a bay system in which a certain type of vehicle, such as the H-Series snow blower or the S-Series concrete mixer, was built in a self-contained area. Today, various models are assembled on the same line, speeding production and increasing efficiency. That new assembly strategy has resulted in less inventory and lower costs. For instance, Oshkosh Truck used to carry five to six days of inventory. It now stocks only several hours worth of components. The facility currently produces 18 trucks a day, compared with eight vehicles using the old system.

–Assembly, June 2000

HOW TO REDUCE COSTS SIGNIFICANTLY

The first step to significant cost reduction is to document present costs. This documentation must accurately and precisely define and detail the costs. Examples of the costs to be determined include:

- Space utilization costs
- Equipment costs
- Warehousing/storage/inventory costs
- Labor costs
- Receiving and shipping costs
- Plant and building costs
- Annual operating costs (e.g., taxes, insurance, maintenance, energy expenditures)
- Manufacturing costs

The next step is to examine each type of cost. For example, an organization can examine its manufacturing costs by asking the following questions:

- What percentage of our manufacturing costs is direct labor? Material? Overhead?
- What costs are included in the overhead? Are they fixed or variable, and are they fairly allocated?
- Are there costs buried in overhead that would be more accurately allocated to materials (e.g., packaging materials)?
- How are material yield, salvage, and waste costs allocated?
- Why do material losses occur?
- How is rework handled? Does this properly reflect the actual cost allocation?
- How is overtime handled? Is this done properly?
- What are the definitions of direct and indirect labor? Can indirect labor be allocated directly to certain products?

An organization should ask questions similar to these for each type of cost identified to understand how the costs relate to one another and to identify hidden costs.

Once the details of the present manufacturing costs are well understood, specific cost-reduction goals should be established and communicated throughout the organization, using the following methodology:

1. Identify unnecessary and duplicate costs, redundant functions, and wasteful spending. This step allows an organization to identify potential areas for significantly reducing costs.
2. Identify and document alternative cost-reduction measures. The organization should consider a wide range of alternatives, leaving no avenue unexplored. Many of these measures should focus on one of the other 11 Requirements of Success.
3. Evaluate alternative cost-reduction measures. To accomplish this step, the company should analyze each alternative economically and qualitatively.
4. Select and specify the recommended cost-reduction measures. This is done by translating the justifiable alternatives identified in Step 3 into an improvement plan that is sold to management and supply chain members and implemented.
5. Update the cost-reduction measures. As stated earlier, Future Capable Company cost reduction is based on the motto "improve, improve, improve." Therefore, the measures cannot be implemented and the process then abandoned. The organization should periodically

benchmark implemented cost-reduction performance against anticipated cost-reduction performance. Corrective action should be
taken when necessary. Most importantly, the organization should
also look for cost-reduction measures throughout the supply chain
on an ongoing basis.

KEEP ON KEEPING ON

The fifth step in the cost-reduction methodology is what separates
Future Capable Companies from other organizations. There are many
organizations that have defined costs precisely and accurately and set
specific cost-reduction goals. However, after they met those cost-
reduction goals, they didn't go any further. The Future Capable
Company is different. The Future Capable company not only bench-
marks implemented performance against anticipated performance and
makes adjustments to the goals, but it also continues to search for
more ways to reduce costs throughout the supply chain. It takes
"improve, improve, improve" seriously, continues to look for the cost-
reduction solution after next, and never rests on its cost-reduction and
profitability successes.

chapter 5

CUSTOMER SATISFACTION

C*ustomer satisfaction is an ongoing, escalating process of meeting customer requirements and exceeding customer expectations. Future Capable Companies must respond to customer needs through customization. They must understand value-added activities, must be flexible, modular, and adaptable to meet ever-changing customer requirements, and must completely comprehend the meaning of high quality while striving to provide high value.*

The power in the marketplace has shifted from producers to consumers. It is no secret that customers are dictating what manufacturers produce, and any company that does not listen will be left behind. Customer satisfaction thus becomes paramount, making it the second of the 12 Requirements of Success for the Future Capable Company.

The basic formula for customer satisfaction is:

$$\text{Customer Satisfaction} = \text{Customer Perception of the Service Received} - \text{Customer Expectation of Customer Service}$$

This formula presupposes two critical statements:

Customer satisfaction is based on customers' perceptions and expectations, not on the company's self-centered view of what the customer may want. (The latter is traditional customer service.)

The level of customer satisfaction will change as customers' expectations change.

Customer satisfaction requires a company and its supply chain to divest itself of self-interest and focus on the needs, expectations, and perceptions of those to whom they provide products. Because customers continuously change while they are customers, companies cannot maintain customer satisfaction with the same set of services and value-adds that satisfied customers yesterday. Supply chains must continually seek information about their customers' needs and expectations, track how they change, and implement processes to address the change.

This chapter discusses customers and introduces methods for continuously improving customer satisfaction.

THE CUSTOMER TIERS

As customers progress in their patronage, they expect more and require more before they are satisfied. For customer satisfaction to remain high, a company must separate its customers into categories, or what we call the customer tiers. Understanding the basic customer tiers enables companies to pursue customer satisfaction in a highly focused and specialized manner. There are three tiers of customers with three corresponding levels of satisfaction.

The first level is the visitors level. "Visitors" occasionally purchase products and services, but have no lasting commitment to the company. To them, satisfaction comes from the fundamental aspects of the product. These customers define satisfaction in terms of product features and costs.

The second level is the associates level. "Associates" regularly, but not exclusively, purchase a company's products and services. Because the associates' experiences have grown since they started out as visitors, their expectations have also increased. They begin to take features and costs for granted and turn their attention to quality. This is a serious challenge because different customers define quality differently. Chapter 11 discusses quality in more detail.

The third level is the partners level. "Partners" are more than customers—they are supply chain partners. These partners have win/win mindsets, team-based structures in place, and communicate with one another on the causes of problems, corrections, and continuous improvement. When an organization has four or five of these supply chain partners, it has achieved SCS. It shares information openly, communicates requirements extensively, and involves alliances early in the process to provide competitive advantage and strengthen the supply chain.

The goal companies should pursue is to transform visitors into partners. Companies must know their customers well enough to evolve with them. They must keep in mind that customer satisfaction grows from a link focus to a chain focus on the ultimate consumer. This will put them in the position to increase customer satisfaction.

HOW CUSTOMER SATISFACTION AND THE CUSTOMER TIER WORK TOGETHER

Consider a situation in which a supply chain produces an excellent product at a competitive cost with high quality, but little extra value is added. Let's say the customer's perception of service was 100 points. If that customer is a visitor whose expectation of service is only 40, then customer satisfaction is high at a 60 (100-40=60). However, if that customer is an associate who expected an excellent product, competitive cost, and high quality and had a point value of 90, then customer satisfaction is only 10 (100-90=10). Or, if that customer is a partner who expected an excellent product, competitive cost, high quality, and considerable value-added support and had a 110-point expectation of service, then the level of customer satisfaction is -10 (100–110=-10). This can be described as a customer dissatisfaction level of 10.

These examples explain why the president of a company with a long history with its customers was having difficulty. As customers' expectations increase from visitor to associate to partner, without a corresponding increase in the customers' perception of customer service received, then satisfaction quickly becomes dissatisfaction. The company thought that customer satisfaction would remain the same if it kept the equivalent level of service or improved it slightly. This was a self-centered view of its offerings. It did not try to keep pace with customers' increased expectations. Thinking that way eventually will position a company for failure.

THE ELEMENTS OF CUSTOMER SATISFACTION

Specific elements define customer satisfaction. These elements are grouped in three categories: pretransaction, transaction, and posttransaction. The pretransaction elements are:

- Nonavailability advisement
- Quality sales representations
- Monitored stock levels
- New product and package development consults
- Target delivery date communications
- Regular product depth and breadth review
    The transaction elements are:
- Ordering convenience
- Order acknowledgement
- Credit terms offered
- Questions handled
- Frequent deliveries
- Order cycle time and reliability
- On-time deliveries
- Order status information
- Order tracking capabilities
- Fill rate percentage
- Shipment shortage
- Back order percentages
- Product substitutions
- Emergency order handling
    Posttransaction elements are:
- Invoice accuracy
- Returns and adjustments
- Well-stacked loads
- Easy-to-read packaging
- Quality packaging
    If a supply chain offers these elements, then it is on the path to customer satisfaction. Offering these elements demonstrates that the demassification of products, rather than mass production, will be a driver of exemplary customer satisfaction. They allow the customer to be the co-creator of value, and they promote ongoing customer dialogue. They also indicate that the company believes that it is good

business to treat customers as individuals rather than as demographics.

HOW TO INCREASE CUSTOMER SATISFACTION

When embarking on the goal of increasing customer satisfaction, a supply chain should first ask and answer one question: "What does our customer want?" The answer to that question leads to more questions, including:

- What do we produce?
- Where do we get the materials to produce it?
- How do we receive the materials to produce it?
- How much do we produce?
- How do we store it?
- How do we package, label, and ship it?
- When do we ship it?
- Where do we ship it?

No one function, or department, or company can answer these questions without help from others. It doesn't matter if your company makes parts and then assembles them or if it has deverticalized to become a virtual factory that outsources noncore competencies, your company cannot increase customer satisfaction without help from your supply chain. Customer satisfaction increases come through teamwork. There must be a positive relationship between internal and external functions. Unfortunately, this usually is not the case. It seems to be the nature of functional areas or companies to be at war with one another, or for suppliers to be at war with manufacturers. Fortunately, a supply chain can end the wars and build a teamwork relationship in three phases:

- Phase I: Cease-fire
- Phase II: Peace
- Phase III: Synergism

The type of company you are dictates how much time and energy must be allotted to this process. However, it is often as difficult to get two warring functions in a company to work together as it is to convince different companies to cooperate. Do not give up hope. It can be done.

LISTENING TO CUSTOMERS: 7-ELEVEN JAPAN

7-Eleven Japan has become that country's leading seller of fast food—even outpacing McDonald's—because its clerks have been instructed to record detailed information on every transaction in their stores. The 7-Eleven clerks not only record what items are sold, but they record the time of day and the gender and approximate age of the customer making the purchase.

7-Eleven Japan stores are smaller than 7-Elevens in the U.S. and cannot keep large amounts of inventory. So, by collecting this information, they were able to tell their suppliers exactly what they needed to satisfy customer demand.

Not only is 7-Eleven Japan's biggest fast-food outlet, but it also is the leading seller of batteries and women's stockings. The company now is the worldwide parent of the 7-Eleven corporation, since it was financially strong enough to come to the rescue when its North American counterpart nearly fell into bankruptcy.

–MSI, February 7, 2000

Phase I: Cease-Fire

The first step in establishing a positive teamwork relationship is to call a truce among all sides, whether they are departments within a company or a series of companies that rely on each other to produce goods. The cease-fire must be mandated and supported by leadership and will be made permanent only after each side understands the other's perspective. Only when mutual understanding truly exists is there hope for peace (Phase II). It is not easy to mold warring factions into a team, but it is possible.

The cease-fire should be mandated as follows:

Step 1. A leadership team sends a memo to the appropriate parties. This leadership team should be created by upper management. The memo must explain customer satisfaction and request that all parties prepare a table that shows their beliefs about other functions and partners in the supply chain. This table should be honest and include stereotypes, each party's view of the others, and the parties' views of themselves.

Step 2. Send each party's views to the others. The leadership team should review all the different views. The leadership team should then identify problems, conflicts, and misunderstandings; establish an agenda to resolve the misunderstandings; and arrange a meeting between all parties.

Step 3. The leadership team initiates the meeting with a description of customer satisfaction and then states that stereotypical views of functions are not acceptable. Each of the identified problems, conflicts, and misunderstandings should be discussed. A positive version of the table created in Step 1 titled "The XYZ Supply Chain's View of Functional Relationships" should be developed at the meeting.

Step 4. The leadership team publishes the chart developed in Step 3 and declares the cease-fire. Upper management has now laid the groundwork for peace (Phase II) and for synergism (Phase III).

Phase II: Peace

Although the leadership team can dictate the cease-fire, it cannot dictate peace. Peace can be obtained only by communication. Although the cease-fire can be ordered in a few memos and meetings, peace is not as easily achieved. There must be an ongoing, long-term commitment to work in unison. This commitment will be obtained when everyone involved understands that their individual successes are tied to mutual success. Either everyone wins or they all lose.

For the process to work, the commitment must be consistent and the communications must be dynamic. Everyone must continuously exchange information on customer satisfaction issues, particularly customization and customer expectations.

CUSTOMIZATION

The new economy has brought us sophisticated customers that demand product customization. The number of options and features that customers require continues to rise, and companies must have the ability to respond. The customers' desires and the costs of various product options must be communicated. Companies that offer those options must help the companies that produce them understand the customers' desires. For example, original brand holders or OEMs must work together to provide the computers and other electronics that customers have indicated they want. They should hold frequent meetings and communicate with one another to satisfy customers.

CUSTOMER EXPECTATIONS

A clear, easily understood, measurable definition of the level of quality and reliability that the customer expects for the price being paid must be communicated to everyone involved in the supply of that product. For example, the quality and reliability expectations of a customer who purchases a $60,000 Lexus luxury sedan are different from those of a customer who purchases a $20,000 Honda sedan.

Likewise, the response time, order sizes, order frequency, packaging requirements, product and package labeling, order audit trails, and shipping modes that customers expect must also be communicated to those involved in production. Everyone must clearly understand the expectations so that they can be achieved economically.

Phase III: Synergism

Phase I results in the end of battles among warring factions. Phase II results in everyone's working together to achieve a common goal: increasing customer satisfaction. Phase III goes beyond working together. In this phase, separate factions become integrated, and increased customer satisfaction becomes a reality.

This synergy is an ultimate focus where material and information flow in a true, top-down progression that begins with the customer. The synergy is both broad and holistic. Business systems are integrated. Products are not being delayed on the dock because no one knows what is in the container. No one is re-entering information that has already been entered by the shipping company. Instead, the partners are using automatically received advance shipping notices (ASNs), cross docking, and vendor-managed inventory. There are no surprises because everyone is focused on the integration of the process for the total good: the satisfaction of the ultimate customer.

How is such synergy achieved? Through a synthesized supply chain. Partners are synergized and energized. Boundaries cease to exist. Everyone sees themselves as part of one huge team working to increase customer satisfaction.

COMMUNICATION IS THE KEY

In each phase of increasing customer satisfaction, communication is mentioned. That's because communication is critical to achieving increased customer satisfaction. When a company, whether virtual or vertical, sets out to integrate business processes and disparate entities, everyone must communicate. It is vital.

Today, there are numerous and varied options for communicating openly—from direct links to virtual private networks (VPNs) that transport data over secure Internet channels as if they were private lines. A wide range of information systems is available for strategic, tactical, and technical purposes. However, this technology is useless unless it creates simultaneous, instantaneous, and multidirectional communications that allow everyone involved to work at the same time rather than sequentially. This eliminates inventory buffers and accelerates the flow of cash. It also allows dynamic planning, which replaces the outdated practices of long-term forecasting. It makes strategic information available to all partners so that all have contact with the customer and are aware of changing needs and trends. They can then respond in unison.

The means of communication is not really important, although the Internet does make these types of communications easier. What is important is using technology to foster teamwork so that everyone along the supply chain can use SCS communications to achieve success. The company leadership must be committed to these open, honest, and clear exchanges, and demonstrate this commitment by practicing open, honest, and clear exchanges themselves.

chapter 6

GLOBAL

B usiness no longer has borders. *The Future Capable Company must realize that success depends heavily on reaching global markets. To reach its full market potential, the Future Capable Company must reach out to other countries and push aside boundaries to promulgate their goods and services. If you are not everywhere, you are nowhere.*

Business no longer ends at the border of a particular country or continent. Trade agreements have been established to ease the tensions and boundaries between once-competing nations. Because of the European Union and the Euro, boundaries between European countries are rapidly disappearing and so are their currencies. The Internet has made the world smaller, and, in fact, has made geography irrelevant. With the speed of information delivery and the shrinking distances that it creates between markets, the supply chains we are competing against may be halfway around the world rather than across town. In many cases, when we are using the Internet to communicate information, we may not even know its geographic destination.

Current trade agreements and changes to laws and regulations, the use and recognition of electronic signatures and authentication, the acceptance of electronic communication, and the promotion of efficient and effective Internet-based commerce have made doing business without borders easier. Companies are using the Internet to serve global markets through:

- Channel management—creating new channels or enhancing existing relationships with channels through better information, speed, and service
- Enhanced collaboration—achieving performance improvement with trading partners through simplified communications
- Market-making—creating new products and services
- Knowledge management—sharing knowledge and techniques across the enterprise and with key trading partners to develop new products and conquer new markets

Interestingly, technology and trade regulations have not actually created the need for a global strategy; they have only simplified global outreach. The impetus for a global strategy is survival. Consider the following:

- The cost of a Future Capable Company's product development is greater than the cost of traditional product development.
- Technology is a critical component of product development.
- Product lives are shorter and shorter.

Because of the above three points, higher product development costs must be amortized over a shorter product life. This can be done by either:

- Allocating more of the product development cost to each unit sold; or
- Increasing the number of units sold.

The first option is unacceptable because it will increase costs. This is contrary to the Cost Requirement of Success. The second option would spread the higher product development cost over a larger number of units. However, with the shorter product life, the only way to sell more units is to expand the marketplace. Today, this expansion can only be global. Therefore, a Future Capable Company must have an integrated global strategy, one that addresses three issues:

1. Global product development
2. Global manufacturing
3. Global logistics

This chapter discusses these three issues and how a Future Capable Company can make a global strategy happen.

GLOBAL PRODUCT DEVELOPMENT

Over the last few decades, there has been a pervasive belief that the United States, Western Europe, and Japan have become a homogeneous market that wants identical products—products such as Coca-Cola beverages, BMW cars, Dell PCs, and McDonald's hamburgers. Those who believe in the homogeneous market concept believe a traditional approach to global product development is satisfactory. Once a product for one of these markets is developed, the identical product is thrown across the pond. The expectation is that a successful product is a product that, without any customization, is applicable worldwide.

Of course, this belief is false, no matter how pervasive. The BMW purchased in Germany is considerably different from the BMW purchased in California. In fact, the BMW purchased in California differs from the BMW purchased in Michigan. Coca-Cola products sold in France are significantly different from Coca-Cola products in the United States. Similarly, in Europe alone, Dell has more than twenty different computer keyboards, and McDonald's serves a different hamburger in Russia than in England.

Thus, the correct definition of a global product is a product that has been developed while considering the needs for global customization, but because of a standardized product platform may be manufactured by lean, flexible manufacturing systems in focused and virtual factories for consumption in the global marketplace. Thus, while certainly not identical around the world, McDonald's hamburgers, BMW's cars, Coca-Cola's beverages, and Dell's PCs are global products.

As customers become more sophisticated, they demand a higher level of product customization. The number of options available to customers is increasing rapidly, and a Future Capable Company must be able to respond to this customization requirement. This trend applies not only within any given country, but also—and even more importantly—among countries. Future Capable Companies must address the needs for domestic and global customization and include the needs for this customization while the product is being developed. Also, marketing, sales, vendors, and customer perspectives must exist for the entire world.

GLOBAL CUSTOMIZATION NEEDED: LUER CONNECTORS

Luer connectors consist of tapered barrels and a conical male part that fits into it without a seal. The original purpose of the Luer fitting was to connect a hypodermic needle to a delivery tube. However, it has been so successful as a connector that it is being used widely in other medical devices around the world, raising possibilities of wrong connections that could have fatal consequences.

Because its popularity was not expected or planned, The European Committee for Standardization (CEN) has had to intervene. CEN has issued recommendations to avoid dangers from incorrect use of Luer connectors between medical devices. In the future, CEN recommends, Luer connectors in use today should be restricted to devices leading to the vascular system or a hypodermic syringe. Connectors used for devices linked to the digestive tract or the respiratory system, or other uses, should be designed so they are not directly compatible with those Luer connectors used for the vascular system.

–Global Design News, June 1, 2000

GLOBAL MANUFACTURING

Global manufacturing can be viewed from the perspectives of offshore global manufacturing and global networks. The following examples illustrate each of these perspectives.

Offshore Global Manufacturing
In an effort to reduce the costs of manufacturing, an electronics company had decided to have its printed circuit boards assembled and tested in Korea. The company made a common mistake and compared its fully burdened in-house standard cost of the board to the unburdened, offshore standard cost. The annual production forecast was for one million printed circuit boards and had a fully burdened

in-house standard cost of $6.54. An analysis resulted in the unburdened, offshore cost for the printed circuit board of:

F.O.B. Cost	$4.02
Overseas Buying Commission	.09
Duty	.65
User Fee	.08
Ocean Freight	.21
Insurance	.04
Broker Charge	.11
Subtotal: Landed U.S.	$5.20
Inland Freight	.06
Total Standard Cost	$5.26

Management subtracted $5.26 from $6.54 and decided there was a $1.28 per unit savings. This savings for one million units translated into an annual savings of $1,280,000 and the decision was made to ship the printed circuit boards to Korea.

A year later, a study was done indicating that although the printed circuit boards were being purchased for $5.26, there was no real savings. In fact, an increased burden existed for the remaining products in the plant. This surprised management, who then commissioned a study of burden. The study concluded that the increase in burden was attributed to the following factors:

- Inventory—Less responsiveness and longer transport times resulted in both transit and in-plant inventories increasing.
- Purchasing—The physical separation, monetary fluctuations, and language difficulties resulted in increased purchasing cost.
- Receiving—Transport interface problems, paperwork problems, and non-standard packaging materials resulted in increased receiving cost.
- Communications—Different time zones, distances, and language problems resulted in increased vendor communications cost.
- Exceptions—The long distances involved and the difficulty with overseas transport resulted in increased costs of handling damaged, missing, or incorrectly labeled goods.
- Quality—The long distances involved and the difficulty of commu-

nicating expectations and changes in expectations resulted in increased quality costs.

- Environment—The managerial frustration of dealing with different cultural, legal, and political factors resulted in a loss of efficiency and, thus, increased administrative costs.

An assessment of these costs resulted in a fully burdened offshore unit cost of $6.80 or $.26 per unit more than the fully burdened in-house cost per printed circuit board. Although management thought they would save $1,280,000 by shipping the printed circuit boards offshore, what occurred was increased costs of $260,000.

The lesson to be learned from this example is that burden does not disappear when products are shipped offshore. In fact, shipping products offshore often increases burden. Therefore, the cost savings potential of shipping products offshore is often more myth than fact.

Global Networks
Global manufacturing is a network of Future Capable Companies. The networks of operations evolve as demand expands. The decision to expand an existing facility or build a new facility typically depends upon transportation costs, factory investment costs, and overhead costs. As transportation costs increase, the tendency is to have more, smaller-volume facilities. As facilities investment and overhead costs increase, the tendency is to have fewer, higher-volume facilities.

DEVELOPING A GLOBAL STRATEGY

The first step in developing a global strategy is to answer one question: Do we have a global supply chain in place? The answer to this question is critical. A global supply chain is a core component of a successful global strategy.

If your company has a global supply chain in place that was developed by applying strategic planning methodology to the supply chain design, then you are ahead of the game. A strategic supply chain plan meets a specific set of requirements over a given planning horizon. A good plan determines the best supply chain for providing the customer with the right goods in the right quantity at the right place at the right time and minimizes the total supply chain cost. The objective of supply chain planning is minimizing inventory while establishing the most economical way to ship and receive product, while also maintaining or increasing customer satisfaction. More simply, the objective is to maximize profits and customer satisfaction.

Strategic supply chain planning typically answers the following:

- Who should we partner with to create our supply chain?
- How many factories and distribution centers (DCs) should exist?
- Where should the factories and DCs be located?
- How much inventory should be stocked at each DC?
- Which customers should be serviced by each DC?
- How should the customers order from the DC?
- How frequently should shipments be made to each customer?
- What should be the service level?
- What transportation methods should be utilized?

Preparation for the global supply chain plan should include preparing answers to the following questions:

- Who are our global supply chain competitors? What are their strengths and weaknesses? What are their present markets? How do they operate? What impact do these global competitors have on our market?
- How do our competitors' products differ from ours? What are the differences in global customers? What are the global pricing differences?
- What are the latest trends in global customization? Are we on top of these?
- What is the global demand for our products? How will this change during the next five years? What companies have what percent of each market?
- Do constraints, restrictions, or barriers affect the free trade of our products around the globe? How will this change during the next five years?
- How can we continue to increase our participation in the global marketplace?
- What are the risks (if any) associated with the global marketplace? How could we minimize them?
- What weaknesses do we have that could negatively affect our global strategy?
- What global strengths do we have? Are they fully utilized? How else could we benefit from them?

If a company does not have a global supply chain based on strategic planning, the steps to correct the situation are:

1. Document the present supply chain and costs
2. Identify customer satisfaction requirements
3. Establish database
4. Develop alternative supply chains
5. Model annual operating costs
6. Evaluate alternatives
7. Specify the plan

Planning a supply chain is a sequential process that continually needs updating. Some companies run into the pitfall of performing steps 3 through 6 before collecting information for and understanding the most important steps, which are 1 and 2. The answer to supply chain planning is only as good as the understanding of the requirements and opportunities for improvement.

Documenting the present supply chain and its costs, identifying customer satisfaction requirements, and establishing the database can be done simultaneously. The main goals are to gain an understanding of the current supply chain and to define the requirements of the future supply chain. To document the existing systems, the following information needs to be collected for each supply chain link:

- Space utilization—determine the size and the space utilization of each facility.
- Layout and equipment—list the equipment and layout of each facility.
- Operating procedures—understand the methods and procedures. Understand the differences in operating methods between facilities. This benchmarking will allow a company to understand better the opportunities for improvement.
- Staffing levels—document levels by position. Understand which jobs could be consolidated. Collect labor rates by level, including fringe benefits. Understand different global labor practices (vacation, holidays, severance, etc.) to understand global staff utilization and capacities.
- Activity levels—understand the volume of activity performed at each facility and the capacity of each operation.
- Building characteristics—collect building characteristics such as clear height, lighting levels, and column spacing. Collect this for the

same reason as layout information, but keep in mind expansion capabilities.

- Access to location—review the access to transportation. Determine the constraints and opportunities for each facility.
- Annual operating cost—collect lease cost, taxes, insurance, maintenance, energy costs, and other facility costs.
- Inventory—collect information on inventory turns and levels, fill rates, safety stock levels, and ABC analysis. By having this information, the savings of consolidating facilities can be determined. Also learn which and how much stock is slow-moving or seasonal to help determine if it should be centralized in one location or if third-party logistics providers should be considered. Establish future inventory goals.
- Performance reporting—understand the performance measures for each facility.

The following information should be collected for the transportation system:

- Freight classes and discounts—collect the freight classes and rates used. In addition to freight classes, get the discounts by carrier. It is also important to understand where the discounts apply and under which parameters (i.e., routes, minimum weights).
- Transportation operating procedures—understand how a certain mode of transport is selected and how a carrier is selected.
- Delivery requirements—what are the delivery requirements to the customer in days, and how is carrier performance measured?

At the end of the site visits, a project team meeting should be held that summarizes the data collected and the assessment of each site. This assessment will give the team insight into the operation, and more than likely they will discover information unknown to management that will be useful in developing alternatives.

To document future supply chain requirements, it is not only important to understand the factors influencing logistics but also to understand the marketing strategies and sales forecast. The following list identifies questions that marketing and sales should answer:

- Are there any new products being planned? From where are they sourced? What is the target market area (geographically)?
- What are the ordering parameters right now? For example, what is the minimum order size? Are suppliers changing any terms of order

(i.e., charging for expedited service)?
- What is the direction of the market (packaging changes, whole-salers, mass merchants having more volume)?
- What is the sales increase each year?
- Are customer shifts becoming apparent? Are fewer customers handling more volume?
- Have geographic shifts emerged? Have sales increased by geographic regions?

One of the key data requirements in analyzing a supply chain is that of the delivery requirements (time from order placement to receipt of the shipment). If the requirements are known, a customer satisfaction gap analysis must be undertaken. The gap analysis is a series of questions directed at both internal staff and customers. The purpose is to identify discrepancies between customer perception of satisfaction and satisfaction requirements. At some point, sales sharply decline because competition exceeds both your delivery and your cost (assuming equal product quality). The key is to maintain a high level of customer satisfaction while maximizing profits.

The database of orders that are to be modeled can be established while the existing supply chain is being documented. This information should include ship-to locations, weight of the shipments, products ordered, and the quantity ordered. Once the data is established, the next step should be to validate the data. Also, it is a good idea to prepare a summary report (sales, cases sold, weight shipped) for a sanity check to ensure all the data reflects reality. Once the data is valid, various analyses such as ABC analysis by picks, location (geographical), volumes, and product volumes by regions of the country, should be run. These reports should be used to help determine alternatives.

Once the data has been collected, the next step consists of developing alternative partners' locations and operating methods. The input used to determine alternatives consists of site visits, projections of future requirements, database analysis, and customer satisfaction surveys. The methods used for the selection of each alternative will vary. Operating methods must be considered. Consideration must also be given to criteria such as consolidating vendor shipments, centralizing slow-moving items in one place, keeping company divisions separate and direct shipment by vendors. Once alternatives are determined, data must be collected on freight rates, warehouse costs, and labor costs for the alternatives.

Modeling software doesn't guarantee the right answer. It is only a tool to aid in the decision process. The real value in supply chain planning is the knowledge gained from understanding the working of a company's supply chain, knowledge of supply chain planning, and the imagination to use the model in ways that really benefit the supply chain. The overall approach should closely follow these steps:

1. Validate the existing supply chain computer model to simulate the existing cost. Compare this cost to actual cost.
2. Run an alternative supply chain. Once the model is valid, alternative supply chains should be run for present volumes and forecasted volumes.
3. Summarize runs and rank. Create a table to summarize cost by alternative.
4. Summarize all annual costs and customer satisfaction factors. Create a table that indicates by alternative all the cost and customer satisfaction factors.
5. Perform a sensitivity analysis. The sensitivity analysis is based on the idea of setting up runs that vary some components of the data. This could be a cost that is uncertain or has potential to change. By modifying this single parameter, the effect on the run can be determined.
6. Determine all investment costs associated with each alternative. This includes any new equipment required to increase utilization and reduce cost or any building modifications to accommodate changing customer requirements and growth.

The economic analysis compares the recommended supply chain plan to all alternatives. To do it, you must determine all the investments and savings associated with each alternative. Costs such as new equipment, construction, or any building modification should be included.

The result should be each alternative's return on investment compared with the baseline. Once this step is completed, perform another sensitivity analysis. Then, to round out the analysis, perform a qualitative analysis that examines factors like flexibility, modularity, adaptability, customer satisfaction, and ease of implementation. Once you reach a conclusion, establish a time-phased implementation schedule that lists the major steps involved in transferring the supply chain from the existing system to the future system.

The final step in the supply chain planning process is selling the results to top management. Management must be able to see the impact of the strategy on the total business. Not only should this communication express the finances relating to operating costs, but overall sales and customer satisfaction as well.

THE INTERNET ASSISTANT

Like all the requirements of success for the Future Capable Company, the global requirement is no cakewalk. A company must keep its ear to the ground at home and overseas so it can stay up-to-date globally while maintaining and continuously improving its global outreach. Fortunately, the new global connectivity created by the Internet can lighten the burden somewhat. Thanks to the Internet, communications can be sent to any area in the world in real-time. If the Korean company that assembles and tests one company's circuit boards needs to meet with the 3PL transportation provider and the OEM regarding a ship date, it can be done all at once, despite the time differences. If a pharmaceutical company has plants in the U.K., Italy, and Australia, it can use the World Wide Web to exchange data regarding the behavior of certain compounds.

INFORMATION SHARING AS PART OF A GLOBAL STRATEGY: OMRON INDUSTRIAL AUTOMATION BUSINESS CO.

Customers now demand partners that provide harmonized global solutions for use in all of their operations everywhere around the world. To meet these needs, Omron, a Japanese manufacturer of automation components such as relays, sensors, and switches; computer systems for factory automation; and large-scale control and information systems, recently reorganized along functional rather than geographic lines. Omron has R&D,

INFORMATION SHARING

production, sales, and support bases in Europe, North America, Asia Pacific, the Chinese Economic Area, and Japan. Fifty percent of sales for the Industrial Automation Business Company are now outside of Japan.

Using the Internal Company System, Omron has strengthened the relationships between functional groups across borders to promote more universally applicable solutions. Through the Internal Company System, management has been moved closer to the front line and can more accurately identify and fulfill the needs of customers.

Soichi Koshio, the President of Omron explains: "Some companies have experienced initial conflicts in putting global practices into place. For example, what is the motivation for an engineer in one country to provide service for a system manufactured in and sold from a sales office in another country or region? But at Omron, from initial concept and design on, we stay focused on developing total solutions for individual customers on a worldwide basis that includes service and support."

The strategy has greatly benefited Omron engineers worldwide. The information sharing required to provide total solutions means that Omron's engineers everywhere are up to date on all the latest developments. For example, Omron engineers have shared information about new developments in the use of open platforms in industrial automation, a field in which Omron is taking a lead. Making use of Omron's in-house worldwide information infrastructure, they not only accessed data on specs and requirements, but also contributed to this knowledge base. "This atmosphere is wonderful for our teamwork, our innovation, and our efficiency," adds Koshio.

–Design News, September 20, 1999

The Internet can also help your company:
- Promote a focus on employees as assets rather than expenses; use their knowledge to gain efficiencies or expand markets as they use the Internet to serve on cross-boundary, global teams

- Master customer relationship management through technology investments that link companies in different countries to the ultimate consumer
- Meld together business processes practiced in various worldwide hubs
- Create a place for the customer in the information infrastructure no matter where that customer resides
- Manage virtual structures and create new financial models for them
- Design new compensation plans for employees all across the globe
- Create security for safe navigation across Web-based business communities in different hemispheres
- Leverage various media to create brand and process recognition any place in the world

The possibilities are endless, just as the global marketplace is limitless. If your company has a global strategy that recognizes these two facts and uses them to gain competitive advantage, then it has the global capability to become a Future Capable Company.

chapter 7

SPEED

T oday's business climate may be described in the words of three-time, national, off-road motorcycling champion Chris Stewart: "If you go slow, you will fall." Future Capable Companies must be able to "ride fast," to use BTO, to respond to the customer—to be quick. As John Chambers, CEO of Cisco Systems says: "It's not the big that beat the small, but the fast that beat the slow."

Speed is critical to the success of an organization. That is why speed is one of the 12 Requirements of Success for the Future Capable Company. Today's business environment demands speed. The Internet has created immediate orders, and customers expect their products to arrive almost as quickly. When I talk to clients, one of the comments I hear is, "What we're finding is that people click, and they expect the order ship time—the back end—to be just as fast as the click speed."

SCS, the holistic process of Supply Chain Synthesis, is the answer to meeting these speed requirements, and one of its eight core competencies, Manufacturing Synthesis, is the method Future Capable Companies use to achieve speed in their internal operations. This chapter examines how SCS increases speed throughout the supply chain, and how Manufacturing Synthesis can be used to achieve optimum speed in internal operations.

RIDE FAST OR YOU WILL FALL

As I think about speed as a requirement of success for the Future Capable Company, I see a direct correlation between it and a lesson I learned a couple of years ago, thanks in part to my son. In 1998, my son and I took up off-road motorcycle riding. After a year, he had ridden quite a bit and was pretty good. I, however, had ridden approximately ten hours, and my proficiency did not approach his. I did not let that stop me when he suggested we go to the Sequoia National Forest for an off-road trip he had discovered on the Internet.

Our tour group consisted of national champions—young, strong riders, great riders—and Jimmy and me. Jimmy proved to be a natural and was soon going up and down the mountains with the best riders. I was another story. I was 20 years older than the other riders, I was 12,000 feet above sea level, I had ten hours of motorcycle experience, and I was in the mountains.

After the first day, Chris Stewart, a three-time, national off-road motorcycle champion, sat down with me and made three observations:

- He was a more experienced motorcycle rider than me.
- He knew the mountains and had more experience riding off-road than me.
- He had fallen off a motorcycle more than me, and had many more broken bones and injuries as a result of these falls than me.

He then said, "Ride fast! If you go slow, you will fall. The steeper the incline, the bumpier the road, the faster you must ride or you will fall."

"If you go slow, you will fall," applies equally to business. Companies, particularly those traveling over steep inclines and bumpy roads, must be able to "ride fast," to utilize BTO, to respond to the customer—to be quick.

A company that implements SCS will see response times and lead-times reduced, and they will respond quickly to the marketplace. Why? Because SCS allows—through partnerships, communication, distribution synthesis, and Manufacturing Synthesis—the design of multilevel networks. These networks are complex entities comprising several partnerships, some of which may be outsourcing and third-party firms. They are also flexible, meeting various customer satisfaction requirements. Robust design methods enabled by real-time decision tools should be the source of this flexibility, and they should support distribution and manufacturing synthesis.

For example, a company used a multilevel network to meet the demands of two large companies with long lead-times and small regional firms that needed products delivered within 24 hours. The company created three full-stocking DCs and then set up multiple cross docks located near the small companies for fast-moving products.

MANUFACTURING SYNTHESIS

Manufacturing synthesis combines Lean, agile, and cellular manufacturing to reduce lead-times. Long lead-times make it impossible to plan and control priorities. Shorter lead-times clear the shop floor of WIP inventory, conflicting manufacturing priorities, and other manufacturing problems.

The reduction in lead-time for a company depends upon the historical approach to lead-time and the amount of product customization. For example, the less customization in a product, the greater the opportunity for lead-time reduction. In the age of mass production, reducing customization to reduce lead-time made sense. However, in this age of BTO and customization, relying on less or no customization is no longer viable. Instead, companies must reduce lead-times and increase speed while relying on customization to satisfy customers. The elements of manufacturing synthesis—Lean, agile, and cellular manufacturing—can accomplish this.

For example, Lean Manufacturing:
• Decreases inventory
• Decreases the floor space required to make a product
• Decreases scrap and rework
• Decreases lead-time
• Decreases changeover time
• Increases productivity
• Improves employee involvement, motivation, and morale.

It accomplishes these changes through a series of flexible processes that allow the manufacture of products at lower cost. It is lean because, when compared to mass production, it uses less of everything. It eliminates nonvalue-added waste in the production stream, and its theoretical objective is a lot size of one.

The elements of Lean Manufacturing include:

- Equipment reliability—equipment that runs when needed.
- Process capability—processes that always produce quality.
- Continuous flow—the material flows in small lots through production.
- Error proofing—ways to prevent the product from being built incorrectly.
- Stop-the-line quality system—if items of poor quality are appearing on the production line, the line is stopped.
- Kanban system—a pull material flow system that pulls materials through the production process based on customer demand.
- Visual management—when fully utilized, a new employee can understand how to do a job from the visual information in the plant, and all employees understand the performance of the plant.
- In-station process control—each workstation has the information and equipment for the worker to inspect and produce good quality parts.
- Quick changeover—a system to quickly change from one product to another.
- Takt Time—production is paced to customer demand. Takt Time equals the time available to produce a product divided by the number of parts that the customer wants to buy.

These elements help eliminate waste, and cutting waste is the foundation of Lean Manufacturing. Waste is defined as "anything that consumes material or labor and that does not add value to the final product that is received or purchased by the end customer." When waste is removed from all manufacturing processes, then speed is increased.

Agile manufacturing builds on Lean Manufacturing principles. Agile manufacturing was developed in response to a number of issues:

- Fast and unpredictable turbulence in the marketplace
- The demand for high quality, low volume, and short product life cycles
- The decline of mass production
- Customer satisfaction
- Demands for high levels of value-added services
- Products that are rich in information
- A focus on people and relationships

Agile manufacturing has four underlying principles: delivering value to the customer, being ready for change, valuing human knowledge and skills, and forming virtual partnerships. Its characteristics include:

- Customer enrichment
- Competitiveness through cooperation
- Organizational focus on change and uncertainty
- A highly educated and empowered workforce
- Emphasis on the customer as an individual
- Relationship-driven partnerships
- Flexible management structures
- Virtual corporations
- Products and services rich in information
- Integration

Two critical elements of agile manufacturing are flexibility and modularity. To review the discussion in Chapter 3, flexibility means a variety of items can be manufactured with little or no change in procedure or methodology. Modularity means that manufacturing is capable of producing different volumes of items with little or no change in procedure or methodology.

Cellular manufacturing helps companies reduce WIP and respond to change more quickly, both of which are goals of Manufacturing Synthesis. In cellular manufacturing, group technology principles are used to design efficient cells. Each of these cells is focused on producing "families" of parts. The parts continually flow through the cell in process sequence, from start to finish, without ever leaving the cell. Process sequences maximize the layout, resulting in smaller batch quantities that run through the cell with little material handling and small WIP inventories, creating shorter lead-times.

CELLULAR MANUFACTURING: LUCASVARITY

LucasVarity, an Antilock Braking System (ABS) manufacturer uses cellular manufacturing to assemble ABS

Continued

CELLULAR MANUFACTURING *Continued from page 69*

control modules. The assembly line is broken into two cells that are then broken into zones in which a group of operations is performed. Each zone has its own conveyor to link its stations, but neither the zones nor the cells are linked to a continuous system. Instead, the cells run in parallel so that if a machine goes down, the remaining equipment can handle the load.

The cellular line redesign has proven its worth in operation on the main line at Fowlerville, Michigan. For example, when testing proved to be a bottleneck, it was relatively simple to insert a second test station to solve the problem. In another case, inserting two wire rings at a single station proved to be a bottle-neck. Reconfiguring the line to include two stations solved this—a single ring is inserted at each station and process flow is rerouted.

The cellular nature of the system components makes such changes easy. Only four connectors are needed to add a station. Routing changes can be made from the main panel, which simplifies prototype runs and equipment maintenance. Unlike convention-al systems that may take months to install and debug, the main-line components were up and running within three days of their arrival.

–Assembly, June 1999

Manufacturing Synthesis reduces three types of lead-times: customer lead-time, production lead-time, and manufacturing lot time. The sections that follow define these lead-times and suggest ways to reduce them.

CUSTOMER LEAD-TIME

Customer lead-time is that time between customer ordering and customer receipt. Reducing production lead-time reduces manufacturing lead-time, which reduces customer lead-time. For a Future Capable Company to reduce customer lead-times significantly, its methodology for doing business must change.

The procedures to follow are:

1. Document present customer lead-time
2. Perform a global competitive analysis
3. Establish goals
4. Identify bottlenecks
5. Create teams to eliminate bottlenecks

Documenting present customer lead-times means first gathering data from a number of sources within the organization. Then, the data should be used to create a flow chart with the times recorded for each activity. This flow chart should accurately document actual occurrences, not standard operating procedures. Hard data is necessary if a company is truly dedicated to reducing customer lead-times.

Analysis requires research and study. An organization should research its competitors' customer lead-times. It should also study its partners' customer lead-times. This research should be global. The more a company can learn about what its partners and competitors are doing and how lead-times differ globally, the better prepared it will be when it sets its lead-time reduction goal. Comparing data, creating charts, and conducting gap analyses are all excellent methods for analysis.

The organization's leadership should initiate and guide the establishment of lead-time reduction goals. These goals should include a commitment to reducing customer lead-times by analyzing the flow chart that documents present customer lead-time and rethinking the methods of doing business. Therefore, these goals should be more detailed than a statement that says, "Let's cut customer lead-time from five weeks to three days." This can be accomplished by recording the goals for each activity on the flow chart. The total of goals for each activity should surpass the reduction required to achieve the overall goals.

Bottlenecks are the constraints that lengthen the time of an activity and create longer lead-times. Customer lead-time should be used in the identification process. Many activities on the chart could have bottlenecks. Once they are identified, a series of customer lead-time reduction teams should be chartered to eliminate bottlenecks and reduce lead-times.

Customer lead-time reduction teams should be broad-based and made up of individuals who focus on specific sets of activities. These teams should have the authority to change business methods to achieve lead-time goals. They should also emphasize:

- Simplification of products, processes, organizational structures, systems, procedures and methods
- Teamwork through the elimination of all boundaries and clear and straightforward communications
- Certainty through clear schedules and a disciplined, predictable approach

Short customer lead-times make it possible to control and plan priorities. Reducing customer lead-times will create lower inventories and quicker customer response. Reducing customer lead-times increases speed.

PRODUCTION LEAD-TIME AND MANUFACTURING LEAD-TIME

Production lead-time is that time from the ordering of all materials for item production until the last manufacturing operation is complete. Manufacturing lead-time is that time from material availability at the first manufacturing operation until the last manufacturing operation is complete. The two are intertwined, because the keys to reducing manufacturing lead-time—reducing lot sizes and reducing setup times—also reduce production lead-time.

Lot sizes should be reduced as follows:

1. Document present lot sizes.
2. Identify specific lot sizes for reduction.
3. Calculate the economic lot size.
4. Reduce setup times by following the Toyota Motor Corporation technique and concepts.
5. Identify alternative methods for handling the economic lot size between operations.
6. Evaluate alternative methods for efficient material handling.
7. Justify the investment required to reduce setup times and to efficiently handle materials, with the savings resulting from the reduction in lot size.
8. Define and obtain support for specific improvement plans.
9. Implement the reduced setup time and the material handling equipment as justified and begin production of reduced lot sizes.

Most of these steps are self-explanatory, but two—calculating economic lot sizes and reducing setup times—require further explanation.

CALCULATING ECONOMIC LOT SIZES

The traditional approach to economic lot sizes says that the lot size that is most economical is the one in which the setup cost equals the inventory carrying cost. This tradeoff is logical because as the production lot size becomes larger, the required number of setups is reduced, and, thus, the cost of setup is reduced and the inventory carrying costs become larger.

The traditional approach has been to continually define increasingly sophisticated mathematics to determine the optimal economic lot size. However, a look at the most basic mathematics to determine economic lot size is sufficient.

The setup cost for a year is simply the cost per setup (S) multiplied by the number of setups per year. If the annual usage of an item is (A) items, and the economic lot size is (Q), then the number of setups per year is A÷Q. Thus, the setup costs for a year are AS÷Q.

The inventory carrying cost for a year is the cost of carrying inventory (I) multiplied by the average value of items in inventory. The average inventory level over a year's time (assuming demand is constant and replenishment occurs when inventory is depleted) is one-half of the economic lot size; that is Q÷2. If the unit cost of an item in inventory is C, then the inventory carrying cost for a year is ICQ÷2.

Therefore, recognizing that the economic lot size occurs when the setup costs equal the inventory carrying costs, the economic lot size occurs when:

$$\frac{AS}{Q} = \frac{ICQ}{2}$$

Cross multiplying,

$$2AS = ICQ^2$$

then,

$$Q^2 = \frac{2AS}{IC}$$

or the traditional lot size equation:

$$Q = \sqrt{\frac{2AS}{IC}}$$

The difficulties with the economic lot size equation result from the following:

- The assumption that demand is constant and replenishment will occur when inventory is depleted
- The assumption that the annual usage of an item is accurately known
- The assumption that the setup costs, inventory carrying costs, and unit cost of an item in inventory are known

At best, the annual usage is a forecast, the setup costs and inventory carrying costs are estimates, and the unit cost is a guess. Thus, the economic lot size calculation is the square root of a forecast times an estimate, divided by an estimate times a guess. It is truly interesting when this level of precision results in an economic lot size with accuracy of two decimal places.

The sophistication of the economic lot size formula and the precision of the economic lot size mathematics are not important. What is important is to understand that the traditional economic lot size methodology is a valid portion of Manufacturing Synthesis when specific factors are used in the equation. These factors are:

- A = Annual usage. This is a range of annual forecasts, typically an optimistic forecast and a pessimistic forecast. This range of forecasts will result in a range of economic lot sizes. The economic lot size selected should be the lot size within the range that best conforms to the material handling system requirements. That is, if the calculated range for Q was 7.6 to 15.3 parts per lot and 12 parts nicely fit into a standard tote pan, then the economic lot size would be 12.
- S = Cost per setup. In Future Capable Companies, manufacturing setup costs will be low.
- I = Inventory carrying costs. Traditionally, the value used as the cost of carrying inventory has been 25 percent. This is not correct. An accurate cost of carrying inventory is 35 percent to 45 percent. Inventory carrying costs include:
  1. Cost of capital
  2. Space Ownership cost (lease or amortization costs)
  3. Space operating cost (taxes, insurance, maintenance, and energy)
  4. Inventory management cost (labor, taxes and systems)
  5. Inventory shrinkage cost (damage, obsolescence, loss, or theft).

- C = Unit cost. The unit cost of each part will be significantly reduced due to Winning Manufacturing.

REDUCING SETUP TIMES

The concepts developed by the Toyota Motor Corporation to reduce setup are:

- Separate the internal setup (setup activities that must occur inside a machine and require that it not be in operation) from the external setup (setup activities that occur external to the machine and can take place while the machine is in operation). Ensure that all external setup operations are complete before the machine is taken out of production. Only internal setup activities should be performed when the machine is out of operation.
- Convert as much of the internal setup as possible to external setup. By altering the machine or the setup activities, the total setup time can be minimized.
- Eliminate the adjustment process. By altering the machines or the setup, a standard or automatic setting can be established that eliminates the need for adjustment.
- Abolish the setup. Standardizing parts can lead to an elimination of setup. Another approach is to have parallel operations performing different operations and, by switching a mechanism, use only the operations that apply to each product.

To apply these concepts, organizations should standardize external setup actions and machines, use quick fasteners, use supplementary tools, consider multiperson setup crews, and automate the setup process. Reducing setup times makes a reality of high-variety, high-productivity, low-inventory, and small-production-lot-size manufacturing.

PRODUCTION LOT SIZES AND SPEED: SEMPEC PA

Swiss company Sempac SA is using a new concept for producing smart cards that has increased the rate of production, even with differing batch sizes. Usually

Continued

PRODUCTION LOT SIZES AND SPEED *Continued from page 75*

printing companies manufacture the magnetic stripe
cards with premolded card bodies or bodies punched
from extruded sheets, a process that requires several
steps. Challenging conventional thinking, Sempac SA
adapted proven injection molding techniques. Its
process places a chip module and preprinted labels
into a mold, injects a resin, and joins the layers using low
injection pressures and temperatures. They use a poly-
mer with high flow properties, good mechanical properties, and the ability to maintain high dimensional stability that met the stringent ISO standards for smart
cards.

Using this process, Sempac SA can easily change
production lot sizes with virtually no interruption in the
production process. It may be making telephone cards
one minute, and bank cards the next. Moreover, by
using a four-cavity mold and robotic handling, the
throughput rate is approximately 3,000 cards per hour.

–*Design News, April 6, 1998*

SPEED IS JUST THE BEGINNING

Manufacturing Synthesis is the key to maximizing speed within an
organization's internal operations, and a Future Capable Company cannot meet the speed requirement without implementing Manufacturing
Synthesis. However, Manufacturing Synthesis is more than reducing lot
times and applying Lean Manufacturing. Manufacturing Synthesis also
maximizes certainty, achieves balance, and implements straightforward
and transparent control systems. These are the next three Requirements
of Success for the Future Capable Company, and will be discussed more
fully in the next three chapters.

chapter 8

CERTAINTY AND CHANGE

 Future Capable Company must manage certainty by establishing, accepting, and following standards of performance. When activities conform to well-established and clear standards, errors, disruptions, and crises are rare. Change is expected and is responded to smoothly.

In the Future Capable Company, nobody believes Murphy's Law. In fact, the norm is the opposite of Murphy's Law: "Everything that happens will happen according to plan." This means maximizing certainty to create quiet, order, and stability so that harmony and continuity will exist in an error-free, disruption-free, crisis-free environment. There is no room in the Future Capable Company for sloppy product development schedules, quality problems, maintenance problems, unreliable employees or partners, untimely vendor shipments, or crises. Instead, the Future Capable Company manages certainty by responding to and understanding Change and establishing, accepting, and following standards of performance. When activities conform to well-established and clear standards, errors, disruptions, and crises are rare. Change is expected, responded to, and understood.

Combining certainty and change is the fifth Requirement of Success for the Future Capable Company. This chapter examines responding to Change in detail and then demonstrates how to maximize certainty.

CHANGE

Change has two primary drivers: people and technology. People are driving change because of our ongoing population explosion. In 1860, the population of the world was one billion people; in 1935, it was two billion. In 1974, the population jumped to four billion, and just 25 years later, in 1999, the population was six billion. This ever-expanding population is living longer and becoming more demanding.

Technology is also exploding. The most dramatic revolution in technology, as I noted in Chapter 1, is that of the Internet and World Wide Web. The Internet is growing and moving so quickly that predicting the future with any real accuracy is impossible.

On the Web, buyers are comparing products, prices, and services and forging new relationships in growing numbers. When these relationships are between vendors and customers, the playing field is leveled. The result is the reduction in the value of branding, which is being replaced with emphasis on quality and high levels of customer satisfaction. Companies keep pouring executive energy into the search for both, as well as overall business agility.

Some of these companies try to manage Change. They will soon be history. To manage means to control, and in today's dynamic environment, companies cannot control Change. However, the energy of Change can be harnessed. A Future Capable Company is an organization that understands change and therefore can harness its energy and respond to it.

How does a Future Capable Company respond to Change? As I stated briefly in Chapter 3, it responds with flexibility, modularity, upgradability, adaptability, selective operability, and automation supportability.

FLEXIBILITY

Flexibility is the ability to handle a variety of requirements without being altered. Flexible organizations are those able to produce a variety of different products without changing the method of operation. Their systems are "soft" and "friendly" rather than "hard" and "rigid." They have focused factories, small production lot sizes, versatile equipment, and multiskilled employees. Focused factories were discussed in Chapter 1, and small production lot sizes were part of the focus of Chapter 7.

Versatile manufacturing equipment that can handle today's requirements as well as future requirements is necessary for flexibility. Consideration should be given to:

1. Adjustable length, width, and depth equipment
2. Variable speed, rate, and volume equipment
3. Future computer hardware and software

Flexibility isn't just about equipment, however. It is also about work and workers. For a company to be truly flexible, it must have multiskilled workers. Training for multiple skills eliminates the barriers between tasks so that workers can:

• Understand the implications of their performance
• Detect flaws in one another's work
• Increase visibility
• Solve problems more effectively

For example, at one company, workers are cross-trained to underscore the importance of teamwork. In its logistics center, all workers are trained to do everything from drive lift trucks to operate computers. In addition to carrying out their position's operational responsibilities, the workers are evaluated on the basis of their ability to provide a high level of customer satisfaction and promote a safe and healthy work environment. All employees also strive to achieve a high degree of enterprise–or entrepreneurship–and continuous improvement in their jobs.

Extreme flexibility is the result. However, there is another benefit: Having employees who can do every job promotes the teamwork and cooperation that is necessary for success. That's the kind of focus necessary for the Future Capable Company.

THE VALUE OF FLEXIBILITY: HOWARD COMPUTERS

Howard Computers, a PC manufacturer, has found the right mix of versatile equipment and multiskilling to handle its production of desktop, mini-, and mid-tower

Continued

THE VALUE OF FLEXIBILITY *Continued from page 79*

PCs. Howard sells the computers to schools, banks, and other business users, as well as to customers needing home PCs. Thus, the model mix coming down the production line at any one time can be varied, as Tony Thornton, vice president, engineering, points out.

"We build six base models. But each base model can be made in about a thousand different combinations of hardware components that can change," Thornton says. Adding one of two operating systems—Windows NT or Windows 98—and then loading all the specific software applications a customer wants, further increases the variety in the mix of finished PCs.

Production starts by pre-kitting the components needed for each PC to be built. Kitting reduces the number of line changeovers needed: Components are pulled from shelving and put into kits. After kitting, the assembly line process begins. Two trays, or minislave pallets, are sent to the first progressive assembly station: One tray holds a kit of parts, one tray transports the PC chassis into which the kitted components will be installed. Individual PCs move through six progressive assembly workstations at the head of the line.

Operators are cross-trained to perform any and all of the assembly steps required at the six stations. Cross-training helps in adjusting workflow. With the ability to man all six stations or by having as few as two manned, or using any combination in between, Howard can further balance the line. With this system and 12 associates and technicians, Howard can produce 200 high-quality PCs daily, and each PC may be very different from the one behind or in front of it on the line.

–Modern Materials Handling, January 1, 2000

MODULARITY

Modularity deals with change in volume, rather than variety. Modular operations are those that can produce more or less of a product without changing the method. As a result, systems must cooperate efficiently over a wide range of operating rates.

Modularity requires modular facilities, modular-focused departments in all modular facilities, and time modularity. Modular facilities gracefully handle changes in production volumes. They locate all facility services, all material handling between focused factories, and all network communications in a "spine" that runs roughly down the middle of the facility. The spine functions much like the spinal column in a human being; it integrates the circulatory (material handling) and nervous (communication) systems. By consolidating all material into the spine, automated material handling systems are accommodated and AutoID can control all materials entering and leaving focused departments.

Modular-focused departments are established by laying out the departments so that they accommodate modular job assignments. The key to establishing modular job assignments is to avoid trapping workers within inefficient work confines. An excellent method of doing this is to design the department in the shape of a truncated "U" as illustrated in Figure 2. With this layout, none of the maximum of eight multiskilled operators is trapped. Because they are multiskilled, they can add to the modularity by simply changing work assignments.

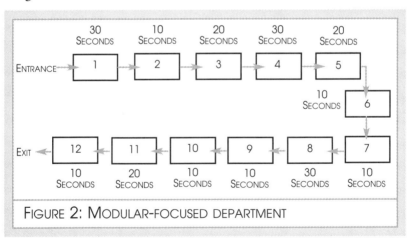

FIGURE 2: MODULAR-FOCUSED DEPARTMENT

Time modularity is creative work scheduling. For example, a focused factory produces at a rate of 100 parts per hour. In theory, the maximum output in a week would be 16,800 parts per week with 24/7 production. The maximum output from one eight-hour shift, five-day-per-week operation would be 4,000 parts. However, if the shift consists of seven hours of work, thirty minutes of lunch, and two fifteen-minute breaks, the five-day work week would produce only 3,500 parts per week. If relief workers maintained the operation during breaks but not lunch, the five-day work week would result in production of 3,750 parts. Thus, time modularity may be used to change production outputs significantly depending on volume.

THE VALUE OF MODULARITY: SCHMERSAL LLC

When Schmersal LLC, a distributor of industrial safety products and switches, prepared to move to a new warehouse in Hawthorne, New York, management decided to replace its industrial shelving with a modular drawer storage system. The decision was part of an overall plan to streamline operations by improving organization and optimizing space. It was prompted by Schmersal's vast inventory growing beyond the shared warehouse walls. This meant outfitting the facility with a storage system that could accommodate current and future storage needs.

Schmersal installed a space-efficient workspace system that consisted of a versatile combination of modular drawers, adjustable shelves and rollout trays, an intriguing solution for high-density storage when floor space is limited. It maximizes storage because it exploits available vertical space. Schmersal installed five rows—one row along the outside warehouse wall and four rows back to back.

Modular drawers that range in height accept partitions and dividers so that Schmersal can store electronic components and accessories of disparate size and shape. The drawers fully extend from the housing, enhancing visibility and accessibility. For faster item retrieval during order picking, all drawers have content labels. Larger parts are conveniently stored on the shelves above the modular drawers. Completing the workplace system are eight industrial workbenches arranged as individual workstations. These workbenches serve multiple functions-from receiving to packaging to housing a UPS computer system to final inspection stations. The space gain in the warehouse is impressive. "The system delivers an overall space savings that will accommodate twenty-five percent growth over the next several years," says Operations Manager Bruce Eylmann." You just can't get that from conventional industrial shelving."

–Modern Materials Handling, January 1, 2000

UPGRADABILITY

The change in business philosophy from "If we build it, they will come" to "They have come, so we must build," demands that systems and processes be upgradable. Upgradability is the ability, to gracefully incorporate advances in equipment, systems, and technology with a minimum amount of downtime. With the accelerated rate of change, it is no longer economical to replace entire systems. Instead, the system should be able to move to the next level without stumbling or hiccupping and with little downtime. Therefore, upgradability is a requirement for any company that hopes to respond to change.

ADAPTABILITY

Adaptability provides the setting for flexibility, modularity, and upgradability. An organization may think that everything it has planned will work. An adaptive environment allows the organization to respond to changes. Traditionally, emphasis has been placed on the control of operations to conform to system requirements at a "steady-state" level. Steady state no longer exists, and averages are irrelevant. Systems now must be adaptive to respond to future system requirements.

Adaptability takes into consideration the implications of schedules, calendars, cycles, and peaks. It allows a system to work well at 9:15 a.m. on a Tuesday during the summer's slow season and at 2:30 p.m. on a Friday during peak demand times. The design, from an operations perspective, must allow a system to work for a one-hour time frame, a two-hour time frame, or a two-week time frame. Adaptability allows an organization to adjust to differing levels of product demand. If an organization builds adaptability into its plans, processes, and systems, it will rarely be caught by surprise.

Through adaptability, organizations identify and destroy artificial barriers. The questions that must be asked repeatedly are: "Has adaptability fully and completely been taken into consideration in all areas and operations within our company? What fixed methods are impeding its progress? What can we do to smooth the path to complete adaptability?"

To answer these questions, an organization should:

- Assess the adaptability of present plans, designs, and ongoing operations. Identify artificial barriers.
- Identify adaptability requirements. Establish specific goals for each of these requirements.
- Identify alternative processes for achieving the specific adaptability goals.
- Evaluate the alternative processes.
- Specify the processes that will best achieve the adaptability goals.
- Define an improvement plan for achieving these goals.
- Obtain support for the improvement plan.
- Implement the plan.
- Audit results and further identify artificial barriers.

SELECTIVE OPERABILITY

Selective operability means operating in segments, allowing for implementation "one segment at a time" without degrading an overall system. This requires understanding how each segment operates. Then, if something goes wrong, an organization can answer questions such as: "How did this take place? What has this done to our level of customer satisfaction?"

Selective operability also allows organizations to put contingency plans in place. A company that locates its distribution center on the North Carolina coast must plan for hurricanes so that other sites are not affected when a power outage, flooding, or roof damage occurs. If the company has a site in Wisconsin, it must be prepared for blizzards so that they do not affect production in a West Coast manufacturing plant. This can be tricky because operating in segments implies that individual links are inherent in supply chain management (SCM). But it is not operating within the individual link as long as the company continues to view the chain as a whole entity. It is only by looking at the flow from start to finish that a company can make contingency plans so that the flow does not come to a grinding halt in the middle.

AUTOMATION SUPPORTABILITY

The future promises more and more automation. Processes and functions that are not automated now soon will be. Implementation will be piecemeal, and nonautomated elements must support this type of implementation. Therefore, it is imperative that all elements throughout the Future Capable Company not only support neighboring elements, but also integrate and interface with them. Integration is necessary for two automated processes, and interfacing is necessary for one process that is automated and one that is not.

It is important to note here that it is easier for a company to respond to change with flexibility, modularity, upgradability, adaptability, selective operability, and automation supportability if the entire organization understands Change.

ORGANIZATIONS THAT UNDERSTAND CHANGE

An organization that understands Change has a number of identifying characteristics. For one, each employee has clearly defined responsibilities, accountabilities, roles, and identities. However, at the same time, not one of those employees is ever heard saying, "That's not part of my job description." That's because the organization does not shackle its staff to outmoded ways of thinking to which they can cling when Change occurs. Instead, the expectations for each employee are delineated and are altered only after conference and mutual agreement.

Another characteristic is continuity and adaptability in the organization's purpose. Organizational focus is proactively, not reactively, maintained. The organization may reconceptualize missions and goals, but it keeps its vision in sight. Also, the focus of employees within the organization is consistent with the organization's focus. However, everyone in the organization understands the necessity of change. All employees believe that Change will benefit them personally and professionally.

An organization that understands Change practices effective communication. Communication is vital to the health of a company that harnesses the energy of Change. Employees are encouraged to participate in and provide feedback about organizational changes. Information flows through the organization in a timely manner.

Understanding change and responding to it puts an organization on the path to maximizing certainty. To complete that journey, though, the organization must also manage certainty.

CERTAINTY

To manage certainty, a standard of performance must be established, accepted, and followed. Before this can be done, however, an organization must define the events that have caused surprises, crises, or changes in plans. This helps determine the standards needed, which include those for:
- Product quality
- Delivery schedule
- Delivery quantity
- Process performance
- Process duration
- Equipment downtime
- Setup duration
- Production methodology
- Part tolerances
- Packaging

Once the standards are established, they must be communicated and conformance to them monitored. The variability allowed in these standards must be considerably less than with traditional manufacturing. Only when tight standards are established and achieved, can certainty be managed.

If there is a lack of conformance somewhere in the company, its cause must be investigated and a plan developed to rectify the situation. A methodology for developing a plan is:
• Identify methods to obtain conformance
• Evaluate alternatives
• Define a plan to obtain conformance
• Obtain support for the plan
• Implement the plan

UNITED WE STAND

A critical factor in maximizing and managing certainty is a united front. Therefore, organizations must resolve to support each other by stating their supply chain's standards and not accepting anything less than that standard. There can be no exceptions. All vendors, organizational elements, and production operations must have the discipline to do it right the first time. In so doing, they all become Future Capable Companies.

chapter 9

CONTROL

F uture Capable Company must practice control with a straight-forward and transparent inventory control system, efficient material flow, and up-to-date and upgradable material tracking and control, while simplifying all processes.

With the unprecedented growth of the Internet, technology, and deverticalization, it is necessary for organizations to strive for control of their supply chains. This is why control is a Requirement of Success for the Future Capable Company. Achieving control can appear daunting, since the accelerating rate of change creates the impression that events are either beyond our control or spiraling out of control. However, with a straightforward and transparent production and inventory control system, efficient material flow, up-to-date and upgradable material tracking and control, and simplified processes, control is possible. This chapter examines these components.

PRODUCTION AND INVENTORY CONTROL

Production and inventory control has been more frustrating and disappointing to management than any other area of business. Millions of dollars have been spent on production and inventory control systems that have not worked.

Deciding the proper direction for production and inventory control is confusing, and terminology fuels the confusion. Much is written about push systems, pull systems, kanban, just-in-time, zero inventories, stockless production, Toyota production and inventory control system, Material Requirements Planning (MRP), Manufacturing Resource Planning (MRP II), and Theory of Constraints (TOC). Unfortunately, the meanings of these terms vary from company to company and from person to person.

Production and inventory control difficulties are an outgrowth of traditional manufacturing. In fact, the complexities of traditional manufacturing have made the effective implementation of production and inventory control systems very difficult. The production and inventory control that meets the control Requirement of Success for the Future Capable Company must be:

1. Part of a Lean Manufacturing process
2. Straightforward and transparent
3. Based on TOC

The results of these elements are vendor and focused department schedules. Adherence to these schedules results in production and inventory control. The following sections briefly explain why.

Production and Inventory Control and Synthesized Manufacturing

A production and inventory control system that is part of a Lean Manufacturing system is radically different from one that is part of a traditional manufacturing system. Because everyone works as a team, the production plan will be more predictable. Because of this predictability, production fluctuations from period to period will be part of the plan. This more predictable production plan and more uniform production rate will result in hassle-free, and therefore simplified, production and inventory control systems.

Synthesized manufacturing, with its continuous flow philosophy, reduces lead-times and production lot sizes. Short lead-times minimize changes in the master production schedule and, along with small production lot sizes, simplify shop floor control systems because less material is on the floor at one time. This all leads to a simplified production and inventory control system.

The increase in certainty and the increase in balance that are also byproducts of synthesized manufacturing make it easy to meet production schedules. Expediting and rescheduling are not the norm. Consistently meeting schedules also simplifies a production and inventory control system.

Straightforward and Transparent Production and Inventory Control

Straightforward production and inventory control is easily understood. Transparent production and inventory control is logical and follows intuition. Both must be based on common sense. Straightforward and transparent production and inventory control involves:

- Defining the products, families, and options to be produced
- Defining the volume of products, families, and options to be produced
- Specifying a production plan
- Defining when materials and capacity should be present to meet the production plan
- Scheduling material delivery from vendors
- Scheduling focused factories
- Monitoring schedule adherence

TOC and Production and Inventory Control

TOC is a management philosophy. Its key premise is that only a few work centers control the output of an entire factory for each product line and that managing these Capacity Constraining Resources (CCR), or bottlenecks, maximizes the output of the factory. TOC utilizes the drum-buffer-rope method to schedule the flow of materials with an eye to market demand and inventory and operating expense reductions. The drum, or constraint, sets the pace of the system; the buffer is the protective window of time that ensures that the drum never runs dry; and the rope is the schedule that releases materials in a synchronous manner and ensures smooth material flow.

By determining the performance limits for all production processes (e.g., recognizing bottlenecks), organizations utilizing the TOC methodology can improve quality and increase throughput.

THE VALUE OF THE THEORY OF CONSTRAINTS: VISTEON CORP

Visteon Corp., a Dearborn, Michigan-based supplier of automotive systems and components, is using a
Continued

THE VALUE OF THE THEORY OF CONSTRAINTS *Continued from page 91*

solution that combines planning systems technology and TOC to address constraints, improve throughput on bottlenecked operations, highlight inventory surplus, and take into account serious demand fluctuations at its North Penn facility in Landsdale, Pa.

The plant must contend with a relatively complex product mix and produces for both original equipment manufacturers and the automotive aftermarket, the latter of which tends to a more unstable demand. "We're able to utilize this system to enable Lean Manufacturing," says Tim Evavold, global business process manager with Visteon. "Essentially, we get the best of both worlds."

According to Evavold, the solution has "virtually eliminated" premium freight charges at the plant and significantly reduced in-process inventories. The planning engine also gives management better visibility to overtime requirements and provides suppliers with a more accurate picture of material requirements.

–MSI, June 5, 2000

EFFICIENT MATERIAL FLOW

Defining the material flow through a Future Capable Company means defining the material and the flow. To understand the material, there must be an understanding of what is moving. To understand the flow, there must be an understanding of where and when something is moving. If a company knows the what, where, and when of a move, it then knows the material flow requirements.

The design of a material handling system is based on the material flow requirements. If you know the material and the flow, you can design the material handling system method, and then you know the how and who of the material handling system.

A major problem for traditional companies and supply chains is that material handling systems are being based on obsolete specifications of material flow requirements like long lead-times, large production lots, high levels of inventory, and unfocused factories. Even a properly designed material handling system based on obsolete requirements will result in efficient material handling systems with the wrong material flows. In a Future Capable Company, the emphasis must first be put on establishing the correct material flow requirements and then, and only then, should the material handling system be designed.

Future Capable Company Material Handling Systems Design
An essential ingredient in designing a Future Capable Company material handling system is to separate the traditional material flow requirements from those of the Future Capable Company. The best method of determining the latter is through the liberal use of the question "why?" The insertion of "why?" in the material flow equation looks like this:

{WHY (WHAT + WHERE + WHEN)} => (HOW + WHO)

The multiplication of the WHAT + WHERE + WHEN by WHY indicates the need to ask the following questions for each material flow requirement:

- Can the move be eliminated?
- Can the move be combined with another move?
- Can the move be simplified?
- Can the sequence of moves be changed?
- Can the unit load be changed?
- Can the material be packaged differently?
- Can the quantity handled be reduced?
- Can the layout be altered?
- Can the move be done as a portion of the operation?
- Can the frequency of the move be altered?
- Is material received in the correct location?
- Is material shipped from the correct location?
- Is the material received or shipped in the proper quantity?
- Is there sufficient flexibility and modularity in the material flow requirements?
- Is a change in the process going to take place?
- Are alternative routings properly considered?
- Are future changes going to impact the material flow requirements?
- Are there exceptions that need to be considered?
- Are there sensitive or unusual aspects of the material to be moved?
- Are there special move requirements that need to be taken into consideration?

While each of these questions is being asked, the summation over all moves should occur. This summation indicates the integration of the methods for each move into a material handling system. Including this summation results in the following Winning Manufacturing material flow equation:

$$\Sigma \text{ MOVES [WHY (WHAT + WHERE + WHEN)]} \rightarrow (\text{HOW + WHO})$$

A questioning attitude is a good foundation and may be all that's necessary to design a Future Capable Company material handling system. However, sometimes it takes a little more effort, particularly since there are obsolete material handling guidelines that may sound sensible, but must be overcome to achieve the true material handling system.

The best material handling is no material handling. When this guideline is interpreted as "Why perform this move?" it should be pursued. However, when the guideline is interpreted as "Since the best material handling is no material handling, I need not be concerned with material handling," no one plans material handling systems, no one budgets for them, and the only ones installed are afterthoughts. This is not Future Capable Company material handling.

The shorter the distance traveled, the better the flow. This guideline makes sense only if the method of traveling the distance is the same. For example, if given a choice between manually moving a load 20 feet or manually moving it 40 feet, 20 feet is preferable. However, if the choice is whether to manually move the load 20 feet or move it on an automated material handling system, the 40-foot move probably is desirable. In other words, the issue here is not how far material travels, but what material handling method results in the least total cost.

Straight-line material flow paths are best. How straight a flow path is has nothing to do with Future Capable Company material handling. For example: would you prefer a move of 30 feet that was straight or a move of 18 feet that was in an irregular flow path?

Handle all loads in as large a unit load as possible. To move a large unit load means accepting large production lot sizes, a large piece of material handling equipment, and large amounts of space. If a pallet of parts is to be moved by a fork lift, an automated guided vehicle system, or a pallet conveyor, then large amounts of either aisle or overhead space are necessary. A more cost-effective method is to break the pallet into a number of smaller unit loads and convey them on a smaller, less expensive conveyor. Smaller unit loads create more responsive and cost-effective material handling systems.

Once traditional and Future Capable Company material handling have been separated and obsolete guidelines overcome, an efficient material handling system should be designed by pursuing these steps:

1. Define the objectives and the scope of the material handling system.
2. Establish the material flow requirements. Verify that these requirements are consistent with Winning Manufacturing.
3. Generate alternative material handling system designs for meeting the material flow requirements.
4. Evaluate alternative material handling system designs.
5. Select the preferred material handling system design.
6. Establish an improvement plan.
7. Obtain support for the improvement plan.
8. Implement the preferred material handling system.
9. Audit systems performance and refine as necessary.

Up-to-Date and Upgradable Material Tracking and Control

To meet the requirements for control, upgradable material tracking and control systems are necessary. A Future Capable Company's material tracking and control system differs significantly from the material tracking and control system in a traditional company. The most significant differences are:

• A Future Capable Company requires real-time, quick-response tracking and control.

• The Future Capable Company's flow requires tracking only when entering or leaving a focused department. This is significantly simpler than traditional tracking, which must occur after each operation.

• With the significantly reduced raw material inventories and the emphasis on customer satisfaction that characterizes a Future Capable Company's supply chain, vendor communications must be real-time. No vendor communications are neglected, delayed, or after-the-fact, all of which are common occurrences in traditional companies.

• To accommodate these differences, the up-to-date and upgradable material tracking and control system must be a simple, real-time system using AutoID, EDI, and the Internet. A material tracking and control system team should be created and given the responsibility of leading the material tracking and control systems efforts. The team should be actively involved with the overall design of the focused department and should have the focused department team actively involved with the material tracking and control system design.

- Before addressing any specific upgrades to the material tracking and control system, the team must define the overall approach to material tracking and control and the overall system's architecture. The material tracking and control system team should take the following steps to ensure an up-to-date and upgradable material tracking and control system:
- Document the present material tracking and control system. Define the present operating procedures and the computer system interfaces.
- Establish a functional specification. In other words, explain the overall operation and the specific tasks to be performed by the updated and upgraded material tracking and control system.
- Within the context of the overall material tracking and control system approach and the overall computer system architecture, define alternative approaches to update the material tracking and control system to accomplish the functional specification.
- Evaluate the alternative approaches. Consider not only the economics of the alternative approaches but also the risk, reliability, modularity, flexibility, ease of installation, response time, maintainability, fail-safe position, and so on.
- Select the best approach. Identify a pilot project to install, test, debug, and refine the updated material tracking and control system.
- Develop a plan to implement the pilot project and a plan to implement the updated material tracking and control system.
- Obtain support for pursuing the pilot project and the updated material tracking and control system.
- Implement the pilot project.
- Audit the pilot project's performance. Provide relevant feedback and make required changes.
- Implement the updated and upgradable material tracking and control system. Audit results to assure satisfaction of the functional specifications.

LOCKHEED'S OUT OF THIS WORLD, REAL-TIME MATERIALS TRACKING SYSTEM

Real-time monitoring is no less vital on earth than in space. After a four-year, $10 million project, the assembly operations of Lockheed Martin Missiles & Space (LMMS) now have their own new system to track and monitor materials for manufacturing. Initial results are encouraging. Lockheed's advanced real-time material system (ARMS) is a third-generation materials tracking system for the company's Sunnyvale, California, manufacturing campus. It's also been developed for rollout to some LMMS remote assembly sites.

The system is perhaps better described as a materials tracking and handling system. It performs tracking activities and ties into automatic data capture and identification technologies such as bar code scanners and printers to do so. But ARMS also carries out a number of materials management activities much like a warehouse management system does. In receiving, for example, it takes care of purchase order and parcel receipt functions along with payment initialization. Material investigation and inspection testing functions are also programmed into the software's suite of receiving activities.

Among its stores or storeroom functions, ARMS oversees stocking, kitting, and disbursing activities. It takes tracking materials up to the shop order prerelease stage. At this point, other systems manage assembly. At several sites it's also tied into automated systems, including one that has a two-tier, 24-pod horizontal carousel subsystem for staging parts in totes. There's also an in-transit tracking capability.

Error reduction and improved data integrity are "huge benefits" reaped by the system, says Lisa Cornelius, software engineer at LMMS. Moreover, "Now everyone speaks the same language and uses identical terminology under the new system."

ARMS' return-on-investment figures include a 30 percent labor savings in parts receiving at one unit

Continued

97

Lockheed *Continued from page 97*

and a 20 percent improvement in cycle time for this sub-process. While headcount remains the same for parts disbursing in the unit, cycle time for this activity is reduced 30 percent. Data gathering for program management shows a 50 percent labor savings in this same unit, while cycle time for this activity has fallen, for a 100 percent improvement.

–Modern Materials Handling, May 1, 1999

Stay in Control: Simplify Processes

Control, like all the Requirements of Success for the Future Capable Company, is not finite. The Future Capable Company, with its "improve, improve, improve" mantra, realizes that straightforward and transparent production and inventory control, efficient material flow, and up-to-date and upgradable material tracking and control can always be improved. By continuing to examine processes and simplify them, the Future Capable Company can accomplish this.

Traditional production processes are very complex. The production of complex products through nonfocused departments that are overflowing with inventory is difficult to understand. Materials are released to the floor in anticipation that, in several weeks, finished goods will result. No one person really understands how finished goods are produced. There simply is too much confusion, expediting, and uncertainty and too many exceptions, changes, and deviations to comprehend the manufacturing processes or systems of traditional manufacturing.

Simplification involves reducing complexities and increasing understanding. Simplifying processes then, means streamlining and more clearly understanding them. In the Future Capable Company, processes and operating systems can be easily understood. Sufficient visibility exists not only to comprehend, but to literally watch products being produced. If the 12 Requirements of Success for the Future Capable Company are genuinely pursued, simplified processes are the result. The simpler the processes, the better the control.

chapter 10

BALANCE

F uture Capable Companies must have balanced manufacturing operations that result in drastic inventory reductions. They have no need for large WIP inventories and must achieve balance by determining the cycle time that must be met to satisfy the supply chain requirements.

In traditional companies, the concept of balance is not present. Their objectives are centered on maximizing machine output. To achieve this, several large production lots sit in WIP inventory awaiting machine availability. The focus is on the output of each individual operation. Such siloism prevents balance.

In the Future Capable Company, there is no need for large inventories because setup times are shortened and certainty is maximized. More important than the speed of operations is the balance of a series of operations. For example, if a company's production requirement is 3,000 units per week and it has only 2,400 minutes of operation time in a week, then the cycle time is:

$$\frac{2,400 \text{ minutes/week}}{3,000 \text{ units/week}} = 0.8 \text{ minutes/unit}$$

The company must produce one unit at each operation every 0.8 minutes. If it has a series of operations producing one unit every 0.8 minutes, having one of these operations producing one unit every 0.6 minutes does not increase output. It is not the speed of any one operation that is critical but rather the balance of all operations that will affect the success of the series of operations. Thus, balance is the seventh Requirement of Success for the Future Capable Company.

Balanced manufacturing operations require focus, continuous flow, sequential flow, standardization, and significant inventory reductions. Continuous flow is the balancing of a series of operations to create a continuous, controlled indexing of parts through production. Sequential flow is the unchanged flow of parts through a series of operations. Standardization requires determining the cycle time, elemental time, standard operations routine, and the standard of performance. The significant inventory reduction balance required is centered on eliminating the problems that lead to the creation of too much inventory. This chapter examines these balance requirements.

FOCUS

Balanced operations require focus, which means that all the operations required to produce a family of parts are located in a focused area.

The original concept of focus evolved from the concept of group technology (GT) in the 1930s. The basic approach to GT was to achieve balance and production efficiency by using a team of people and a group of operations (a focused department) to produce a family of geometrically similar parts. The group of operations was integrated by a material handling system and placed into an integrated layout for the production of the specific family of parts.

In the 1960s, the concept of flexible manufacturing systems (FMS) was created as an approach to achieve the same objective as GT. The basic approach was to integrate the manufacturing equipment and the computer control into a system that was capable of producing a family of parts. Although they are often computer controlled, the essence of FMS was the same as the essence of GT. Therefore, the new approach of FMS was not really new, but rather an update of the original focused department concept of GT.

Then, in the 1980s, the concept of cellular manufacturing (CM) evolved. The objective of CM was to achieve balance and production efficiency by integrating production equipment, material handling equipment, and computer control into a focused department to produce a family of parts. The focused departments were called cells, thus the term cellular manufacturing. In reality, CM is no more than a

1980s version of GT and FMS.

The key aspect in all three is to create balance. This balance comes from focusing the operations required to produce a family of parts in a designated area and focusing the management of the department on the combined output of all the operations.

An extension of the focused department is the concept of focused factories, which provide for the balance and support of a series of focused departments. A focused factory provides all resources required to produce the total product. Focused factories consist of focused departments, focused receiving, shipping, material handling, and management.

Focused receiving and shipping often are best accommodated by distributed receiving and shipping. (Distributed receiving and shipping are the opposite of centralized receiving and shipping.) With distributed receiving, material enters a facility as close as possible to the point of use; internal material handling is minimized. With distributed shipping, finished goods leave the facility adjacent to the final packaging process.

Focused material handling should be viewed in layers. Within a focused department, focused material handling equipment will move unfinished parts between operations. Within a focused factory, focused material handling systems will move finished parts between focused departments. At the highest level within a manufacturing facility, the material handling systems will be moving major subassemblies between focused factories. Focused material handling equipment and systems will be dedicated to handling specified loads over defined flow paths.

A focused factory management system consists of all planning, control, and reporting requirements for the focused factory. The focused management system must include:
• Production planning
• Material requisitioning
• Purchasing
• Receiving
• Material tracking
• Production and inventory control
• Financial reporting
• Quality assurance
• Order tracking
• Shipping

The management system for each focused factory must provide for the operation and management of the factory as an independent operation. Balance can be achieved only by providing this level of control at the focused factory level.

FOCUSED FACTORY: CONTINENTAL TEVES

Continental Teves Braking Systems in Morganton , N.C., was built for brake assembly in 1992. Since November 1997, the plant has been a focused factory, with its operations dedicated to the assembly of the Mk. 20 ABS device-both solenoid valve and hydraulic system assembly. Because it supplies systems to DaimlerChrysler, Ford (with these first two accounting for about 75 percent of the business), Nissan, Honda, Toyota, and Mitsubishi, there is an array of variants of the Mk. 20. The assemblies may look the same, but there are more than 80 different types that can be produced, with such things as different motors, different valves, different pistons, different control units. The 720 people in the plant are responsible for producing some three million of these brake systems per year.

As output increases, the company is working on the ways and means to do it without adding equipment. An astonishing example of how this was accomplished with a "less is more" mindset is the fact that plant employees figured out that although there were eight solenoid valve assembly lines in the plant, that was one too many for production requirements. They wanted to eliminate one line.

Dennis White, the plant manager, remembers it well. "When the people came to us, most of us in management were skeptical-at best," he says. "After all, some clever engineers had determined the capacity of the plant, and they specified eight lines." He explains that the design capacity for the lines was on the order of 4,000 to 4,500 units per line per shift. However, by doing such things as focusing on throughput and gate stations and by making modifications to the equipment, the people on the plant floor concluded that

CONTINUOUS AND SEQUENTIAL FLOW

As a general rule, balance can best be achieved by the continuous flow of parts through production. The frequent movement of small unit loads characterizes continuous flow. Guidelines for facilitating continuous flow include:

- Standardize unit loads and material handling equipment to facilitate efficient, effective, and reliable material handling systems.
- Eliminate, whenever possible, intermediate material handling steps between two consecutive points of use by tying operations together.
- Minimize the number of material handling steps between two consecutive points of use.
- Combine material handling with processing so that the exit from one operation most conveniently feeds the input to the next operation.
- When manual material handling is most economical, minimize the amount of manual activity by minimizing walking, travel distances, and motions.
- Eliminate manual handling by mechanizing or automating material handling whenever economically justified.
- Review all floor space and overhead space for effective utilization.
- Integrate material flow and information flow whenever feasible.
- Integrate the flow of materials from distributed receiving to focused factories, through focused departments to other focused factories, and from distributed shipping into one material handling system.
- Be creative in establishing the most adaptable, maintainable, and responsive material handling system.

True continuous-flow balance can only occur when the sequence of parts flowing through a series of operations is unchanged. If the first operation produces the sequence of production lots A-B-C-D and the second operation must produce in the sequence B-D-A-C, continuous flow is not possible. Teamwork and integration throughout the supply chain are required to receive parts in the proper sequence.

STANDARDIZATION

To achieve balance, all operations must be performed with certainty. And, as discussed in Chapter 8, certainty requires standardization. Therefore, a standard of performance must be established, accepted, and followed for each operation, focused factory, and supply chain partner. One methodology is as follows:

- Determine the cycle time. The cycle time is the time available to produce one unit at each operation.
- Determine elemental time. The elemental time is the time required to perform the work elements and consists of operator time and machine time.
- Determine the standard operations routine. The standard operations routine is the assignment of work elements to operations. The allocation of work elements to operations must be done so that each operation can finish all the assigned work elements within the specified cycle time.
- Document the standard of performance. This standard of performance should specify what consistent performance will result from a company's operations, focused factories, and supply chain partners and how they should be operated to achieve the specified performance.

Once established, the standard operations must then be accepted and followed.

SIGNIFICANT INVENTORY REDUCTIONS

Reducing inventories helps achieve balance because such reduction makes it easier for companies to focus on the problems that created the need for them in the first place. No longer can problems hide behind piles and piles of inventory because those piles of inventory no longer exist. Instead, the problems can be easily located and fixed, and operations can run according to plan.

The reduction of inventories begins by documenting the present levels of inventory, which should be compared to whatever industry yardsticks can be obtained. Factors to consider in determining the proper levels of inventory include:
- Industry norms
- Production constraints
- Seasonality
- Customer requirements
- Material availability
- Variety
- Production stability
- Seasonality of customer demand
- Seasonality of vendor supply

Some questions to ask are:
- What inventory turns and levels are desired?
- What fill rates are desired?
- What safety stock levels are desired?
- What products will be seasonal?
- How will we keep slow-moving inventory to a minimum and eventually eliminate it?

REDUCING WIP: OHMEDA

Engineers at Ohmeda, a medical device manufacturer in Franklin Lakes, New Jersey, decided to replace the existing semiautomatic assembly line with an almost 100 percent automated system. They wanted to combine consistent, reliable assembly with automatic product testing. The original semiautomatic assembly line produced quality devices, but at a high cost. It took more than 200 operators to produce 700 units per hour, with additional cost coming from regular rework

Continued

REDUCING WIP *Continued from page 105*

because of stringent product quality standards. WIP averaged 3,000 units at any one time.

Ohmeda engineers decided to take a two-phase approach to the project. Phase 1 was to include all critical operations, but would omit three modules that would be added in Phase 2. This two-phased approach to implementing the new system proved to be the correct method.

Each module is controlled using an independent industrial-grade personal computer. The control software was developed under an operating system that provides a real-time, multitasking environment. The built-in networking capability of the software makes control of manufacturing operations possible. The control software's tasks use a graphical user interface for setting up process parameters, machine station sequencing and pallet tracking, machine protective controls and automatic error recovery, intelligent subsystem and test apparatus interface, and production reporting.

A new line assembles four related products, with easy changeover, on a pallet-based flexible automation system. Each pallet carries one product. Pallets are carried on conveyors between eight operating modules, but are transported through the modules on a cam-operated walking beam that moves pallets to and from shot pins for accuracy. The cam-operated motion is fast and smooth, with precisely controlled acceleration and deceleration. The closed-loop pallet transport system is flexible and can be modified to accommodate changes in assembly floor space. It can also be altered to incorporate future automatic operations.

The results? At 1,200 units per hour line speed, Ohmeda realized a 96 percent yield and an 85 percent efficiency. Labor hours per unit have been reduced 96 percent. Product uniformity is substantially higher. WIP inventory is fewer than 130 units. Total process time is less than four minutes per unit.

–Assembly, January 1999

Based on the best information available and the judgment of an inventory reduction team, specific inventory reduction goals should be established. An audit should be conducted for each inventory reduction goal to determine why the present level of inventory exists. While considering the goal and the audit, identify specific approaches to reduce inventory. Conduct economic evaluations of each approach to certify that inventory, as well as the total costs of manufacturing, will be reduced.

The justifiable inventory reduction approaches must be integrated into an overall inventory reduction improvement plan. Once support for the plan is obtained, it should be implemented. Compare results with the established goals. Once the inventory reduction goals have been accomplished, procedures must be put in place to ensure the continued conformance to these goals. Only with continuous attention will acceptable inventory levels be maintained and continuous improvement be achieved.

BALANCING ACT

The first step in achieving balanced manufacturing is to document present WIP inventory because it is a symptom of unbalanced operations. Once that has been done, the following questions need to be addressed:

- Have setup time reductions been implemented? What is the potential for setup time reductions?
- Have production lot sizes been reduced? What is the potential for production lot size reductions (one-piece flow, lot size of one)?
- Has certainty been maximized? What potential exists for certainty maximization?
- Has focus been implemented? What opportunities exist for the creation of focused departments and focused factories?
- Do production lots continuously flow through manufacturing operations? Are all WIP inventory buffers justifiable? Are WIP inventory buffers high-turnover, low-inventory hesitations in the continuous flow of materials?
- Have the proper procedures been put in place to maximize sequential flow? How can WIP inventory be reduced by implementing sequential flow?

- Have standards of performance been established, accepted, and followed for each operation, focused department, and focused factory? How can the standards of performance be more rigorously pursued?
- Have the just-in-time operational costs been analyzed? Is there a proper understanding of the trade-off between operating costs and balance?
- Have capacity bottlenecks been properly analyzed? Has the issue of balance been properly addressed both before and after the capacity bottleneck?
- If not already answered, why does WIP inventory exist? Are all WIP inventories justifiable?

No manufacturing operation will ever achieve total balance. Instead, your objective should be to achieve greater balance. Answering the questions above will allow you to prioritize opportunities; identify and evaluate alternatives; and define, approve, and implement improvement plans. Combining these activities with continuous improvement will lead to greater and greater balance.

chapter 11
QUALITY

T *he Future Capable Company must reject the various quality crusades and the quality hype of the last several decades and work to understand that quality is the conformance to customer requirements. It must then put a continuous quality improvement process in place.*

One of the most popular business topics for more than two decades has been quality. There are countless conferences, books, and magazine articles that address quality. Books on quality are on the best-seller lists. Companies have adopted a wide variety of slogans and campaigns to stress the importance of quality. Companies have adopted quality as a strategic marketing theme and have spent hundreds of millions of dollars advertising their products' quality. All of these efforts have given virtually every person in every developed nation an awareness of the quality issue.

The interest in quality has gone so far that the American Society for Quality has an online catalog (http://www.asq.org/abtquality/nqm/rrcatalog.html) that offers more than sixty products (this does not include books) that feature the word "quality." The Quality Press catalog advertises books that address 47 different types of quality. Need a desk reference for statistical quality methods? You can order one. Not sure how to implement a nuclear quality assurance program? Just consult the International Matrix of Nuclear Quality Assurance Program Requirements. There is even a company that

109

produces a "Quality-a-Day Calendar" every year.

Quality is more than a fad, and more than a movement. However, because so many companies have adopted a "management by fad" mindset for their quality programs, a certain cynicism regarding quality has developed. For example, a search of an online humor archive produced a number of jokes and humorous anecdotes related to quality. One such anecdote, called Star Trek with Dilbert Management, reflects this cynicism with such statements as, "Data fails an ISO 9000 audit because the construction of his positronic brain isn't properly documented. He curses Dr. Suhn's record-keeping as he's stripped for parts," and, "All members of the ship's maintenance crew are required to be involved in Quality Circles. The loss of productive work time causes them to cut back on scheduled repairs, resulting in a warp core breach that kills everyone."

This cynicism has developed because companies have stressed quality without truly understanding what it is. Everyone is in favor of quality. Everyone talks about quality. Everyone recognizes quality when it is present, but many find its definition unclear, its measurements elusive, and their roles in it uncertain. The secret to clearing up the quality mystery is to ignore the hype and focus on understanding, establishing and improving product, vendor, and information quality; all of which are addressed in this chapter. The Future Capable Company must focus on these things, because quality is the eighth Requirement of Success for the Future Capable Company.

UNDERSTANDING QUALITY

The American Society for Quality's most recent definition of quality is "a subjective term for which each person has his or her own definition. In technical usage, quality can have two meanings: 1) the characteristics of a product or service that bear on its ability to satisfy stated or implied needs, and 2) a product or service free of deficiencies." Many U.S. companies interpret quality to mean conforming to requirements.

Peter Drucker put a different spin on quality. He wrote, "Quality in a product or service is not what the supplier puts in. It is what the customer gets out and is willing to pay for. A product is not quality because it is hard to make and costs a lot of money, as manufacturers typically believe. This is incompetence. Customers pay only for what is of use to them and gives them value. Nothing else constitutes quality." Drucker's definition is similar to the Japanese definition, which says that quality is what satisfies the customer.

There are weaknesses in the above definitions. Drucker and the Japanese identify the customer as the judge of quality, but they do not provide a method of evaluating quality. The American definition offers a method of evaluating quality, but its weakness is that it does not state that quality can only be obtained when the customer establishes the requirements. A combination of the Japanese and the American definitions leads to a precise definition of quality: Quality is conformance to customer requirements. There are specific elements of quality that companies throughout a supply chain must consider in order to meet this definition.

The Elements of Quality

To produce a product that conforms to customer requirements, a company must record eight elements of quality. With a PC as an example, these elements include:

- Performance—The operating characteristics of the product (the speed of the computer, its RAM, the size of its hard drive, its operating system)
- Features—Secondary characteristics that supplement the product's operating characteristics (a CD ROM drive, a CD burner, a Zip® drive)
- Reliability—The anticipated failure rate of the product (length of time before the motherboard goes bad or the CPU stops working)
- Conformance—The lack of defects in the product when delivered (the CPU and monitor cases are properly fitted, the circuit boards are properly placed)
- Durability—The useful life of the product (the number of years before the computer and its operating systems are so obsolete they cannot be updated)
- Serviceability—The ability to obtain satisfactory repair (availability of chips, motherboards, and other parts and the ease of installation of these parts)
- Aesthetics—The customer's feelings about the appearance of the product (how the customer views the way the computer looks)

- Perceived quality—The customer's overall feeling about the product (subjective judgment of the customer as to which is the best computer)

Customer requirements should be established for each of these eight elements. The product that best conforms to these requirements is the highest-quality product.

Quality Control, Quality Assurance, and Total Quality Control

Understanding quality means more than knowing its definition. There must also be an understanding of what is meant by quality control, quality assurance, and Total Quality Control (TQC). These terms are not synonymous. Quality control is the techniques, information, and processes necessary for achieving the conformance of the product to customer requirements.

QUALITY CONTROL THROUGH STANDARDIZATION: JOHNSON CONTROLS

Building it right the first time is not just a slogan at Johnson Controls, it's a multimillion-dollar commitment. To ensure that products built at the company's 265 manufacturing plants throughout the world are uniform regardless of where they're made, Johnson Controls embarked three years ago on a standardization program called Manufacturing, Engineering, Quality (MEQ). Before the company implemented the MEQ initiative, the plants dealt with local suppliers and made whatever arrangements suited them. Because of disparate equipment and discrepancies in the way plants operated, however, maintaining consistency among them was a constant challenge. Sometimes product launches were smooth, and sometimes guaranteeing consistency worldwide required an extra effort from engineering.

"The strategy of the MEQ program is to standardize the equipment and processes in all of the company's plants worldwide. By doing so, the consistency of products can be controlled more efficiently from plant to

QUALITY CONTROL THROUGH STANDARDIZATION

plant," explains Brad Perry, quality manager at the Johnson Controls Center of Excellence (Ann Arbor, Michigan).

Moreover, economies of scale can be gained by working with one vendor to develop and deploy advanced technology.

A major challenge that every plant in the group faces is making sure that all of the bolts in the seat frames and tracks are tightened to the correct torque. "Most bolts in seat frames and tracks are critical to safety, so our customers will specify lower and upper torque limits," Perry says. "The lower limits prevent 'undertightening,' which could allow bolts to work their way loose over time or to dislodge during an accident. The upper limits prevent 'overtightening' a bolt beyond its elastic limit and deforming it enough to yield in use."

To tighten bolts within the specified limits and a Cpk of 1.67, Johnson Controls chose Tensor-S nutrunners from Atlas Copco Tools Inc. (Farmington Hills, Michigan) as its company standard. An outcome of the ensuing relationship with this supplier is the new Power Focus 3000 controller that oversees the nutrunners. Inside the controller is a special microprocessor chip dedicated to nutrunning and TCP/IP network communications. Consequently, the controller can guarantee each bolt is tightened within the customer's design limits without Johnson Controls engineers having to string a maze of PLCs and relays and write complex logic each time they set up a new line.

–Assembly, September 2000

Quality control has three main principles:
1. Quality cannot be inspected into a product.
2.. Quality cannot be built into a product.
3. Quality can only be designed into the product and the processes that produce it.

Quality assurance is the ongoing activity that ensures that products conform to customer requirements. Therefore, quality control occurs before production, and quality assurance is an auditing activity that takes place during production.

The combination of quality control and quality assurance is TQC. TQC puts quality into products, processes, and information systems. For all products, the proper design must occur to control quality, and then manufacturing processes must be audited to ensure quality. The Future Capable Company must understand that this combination of quality control and quality assurance is an integral part of the Quality Requirement of Success.

ESTABLISHING QUALITY

Considerable progress has been made in the quality field in recent years. Although quality is often driven from the top through slogans and elaborate campaigns, quality control and quality assurance are mostly proactive. For example, statistical process control (SPC), a management tool that brings processes into control, and keeps them there, is used to identify process variability due to assignable causes. Therefore it serves as an early warning system for producing unacceptable parts. Through the use of SPC, the costs of poor quality may be minimized and quality may be ensured.

Quality standards such as ISO 9000 and QS 9000 (for the automobile industry) are also helpful tools. They may be used to document processes and conformance to standards, and certification isn't necessary. However, it is important to remember that they cannot be the only tools used to achieve quality—nor can they replace the continuous improvement processes necessary for achieving quality.

Most impressive has been the inroads made in producing quality information. In my 1989 book, *Winning Manufacturing*, I wrote that the requirements for quality information were high-speed processing, reusability, low cost, and simultaneous availability. At that time, I had no idea that an information revolution would take place that would replace my original ideas of how these features could be achieved! The Internet and its various means of communication have made these requirements a reality far beyond my wildest imaginings.

In the Future Capable Company, the methods for achieving quality must continue to be progressive. In other words, quality must be:
• Top-down driven from an awareness and commitment perspective
• Bottom-up driven from a measurement and reporting perspective
• Customer-driven from a requirements perspective

Quality must continue to be a proactive, strategic activity of critical importance for everyone in the Future Capable Company, from the president to the marketing department to the shop floor. Slogans and campaigns must be replaced by quantifiable objectives.

Inspection will often be done of all units, in-line and on a real-time basis. Inspection should be automated. Data should flow to real-time SPC systems for a real-time audit of the process. However, the inspection objectives will be much more than attempting to distinguish good ones from bad ones and collect data for SPC. By being in-line and real-time, inspection will be the hub of the following:

• Process control
• Increased consistency
• Feedback
• Real-time stoppage and the identification of the reason for stoppage
• Predictive maintenance
• Management reporting
• Customer quality documentation
• Feedback to product and process planning

Quality information is critical to establishing quality. Without information, there are no products, no customers, no orders, no materials, no machines, no employees, no supply chains, no anything. It is quality information that makes a company function. Therefore, systems must be put in place to provide for accurate, reliable, consistent, and simultaneous information. Quality control and quality assurance for information are just as important as quality control and quality assurance for vendors and products. Misinformation, like defective parts, must be found, investigated, and corrected so that the cause of the misinformation is eliminated.

How to Improve Product, Vendor, and Information Quality

The understanding of quality and the commitment to quality must be the foundation for a supply-chain-wide quality improvement program. Therefore, based on an understanding of quality, leadership throughout the supply chain must make a strong commitment to quality and communicate it to everyone. In other words, everyone in upper management must demonstrate the commitment through active participation and capital investment.

Once this foundation is in place, the following steps should be taken to improve quality:

- Identify the customer. Know the customer. Understand the customer's business. Adopt the customer's perspective.
- Define customer requirements. Communicate with the customer. Obtain a clear definition of the customer's requirements. Make sure all parties involved share the same customer expectations.
- Assess the supply chain's present quality performance. Document the performance. Compare this performance with the customer's requirements. Identify areas where customer expectations are not exceeded.
- Identify problems. Investigate performance shortfalls. Define the reasons for them. Communicate with all parties involved to understand the shortfalls.
- Specify alternative solutions. Break through communication barriers and traditional constraints to identify creative potential solutions. Be certain each alternative solution solves the problems, not just relocates them. Document the operating characteristics of each alternative solution. Verify that each alternative solution will result in exceeding customer requirements.
- Evaluate alternative solutions. Do an economic and qualitative evaluation of each alternative solution. Identify the best solution to each performance shortfall.
- Establish improvement plans. Translate the selected solutions into an action plan. Obtain support for the action plan.
- Implement improvement plans. Install equipment, train personnel, and debug the installation of the solution. Ensure the solution's performance.
- Audit results. Verify that performance exceeds customer expectations. Install systems capable of ensuring that customer's requirements are exceeded.

For this quality improvement methodology to succeed, it must be a broad-based, participative effort involving upper management, middle management, purchasing, product development, engineering, marketing, supervision, shop-floor personnel, vendors, and customers throughout the supply chain. Everyone who has an impact on quality must be educated if the company is to obtain an awareness and understanding of quality.

QUALITY IS A SOUND INVESTMENT

In the 1990s, the slogan "Quality is Free" became quite popular. This was unfortunate. Why? Because some corporations have taken the position that quality can be improved with little or no investment of time and capital. Of course, these are the organizations that are now scratching their figurative heads wondering why their customers aren't satisfied. They don't understand that their "free" slogans and posters haven't improved the quality of their products.

To establish and improve quality, a significant investment of capital and time by all levels of an organization and its supply chain is required. Quality is like anything worthwhile in business—there are no quick fixes, and financial shortcuts will put you on the road to ruin.

No, quality is not free. Instead, it is an excellent investment that is sure to improve a supply chain's net worth. The Future Capable Company understands this and makes wise investments in employees, process systems, audits, products, and information systems so that consistent understanding of quality is distributed throughout the supply chain.

THE VALUE OF QUALITY IMPROVEMENT: SUPERIOR STAMPINGS

Delphi, General Motors, and other automotive manufacturers require their suppliers to inspect 100 percent of their parts and to guarantee 100 percent quality parts. Steve Morgan, president of Precision Stampings Inc. (PSI), Beaumont, California, has found that machine vision can provide that capability. PSI manufactures progressive metal stampings for the automotive, military, computer, and hardware industries.

In PSI's previous quality control system, operators inspected the beginning and end of each roll of stamped parts. However, this process did not allow the company to guarantee 100 percent quality. If the sample segments passed inspection, the reel was

Continued

THE VALUE OF THE QUALITY IMPROVEMENT *Continued from page 117*

shipped. With up to 100,000 stampings on a reel, problems that occurred in the middle of a run went unseen. A system that could detect those defects was necessary if PSI was to guarantee 100 percent quality parts. After attending a trade show in 1998, Morgan purchased a machine vision system manufactured by PPT Vision Inc. (Eden Prairie, Minnesota). PSI die makers resisted using the system at first. They wondered why the company wanted to spend time and money changing an already successful process. Morgan finally convinced one die maker to try the system, off-line in a separate room. That die maker was impressed with the results, and now all 18 die makers are willing to implement it.

The PPT machine vision system inspects 100 percent of the stampings as they move off the press and onto the reel, allowing PSI to guarantee 100 percent quality parts. The first defective part causes the vision system to shut down the press and alert the operator, who then corrects the problem and removes the defective part from the reel. This system eliminates scrap and rework. Charts and graphs are generated by real-time statistical process control programs. Operators then can monitor the process for potential problems and adjust production equipment before it produces nonconforming parts or has to be shut down for repairs. By implementing the PPT system, PSI has decreased scrap, maintenance time, and replacement parts, while increasing tool efficiency and the expected life span of equipment.

–Assembly, September 2000

chapter 12

MAINTENANCE

T he Future Capable Company must fully understand the scope
of physical asset management and the maintenance process.
Maintenance for the Future Capable Company combines reliability, predictive maintenance, and preventive maintenance
to create high levels of uptime and productivity, anticipate
potential problems, and minimize future problems.
Maintenance and operations must be integrated and function
as a supportive team through improved planning, scheduling,
and cooperative team-based continuous improvement efforts.

In many organizations, the maintenance function does
not receive proper respect. The naïve perception is that
maintenance does not add value to a product, and thus,
the best maintenance is the least costly. Armed with this
false perception, traditional manufacturing companies
have:
- Underemphasized preventive, corrective, and routine
  maintenance
- Not addressed predictive maintenance and reliability
  improvement
- Not properly trained maintenance personnel
- Not properly developed effective maintenance leadership

Maintenance is not an insurance policy or a security
blanket; it is one of the Requirements of Success for the
Future Capable Company. Without effective maintenance,
machines and systems will fail. When failure occurs, the
following will happen:

- Uncertainty will be the norm. The Requirements of Success state that certainty must be maximized.
- Balance will not be obtainable. The Requirements of Success state that all operations must be balanced.

The Future Capable Company cannot tolerate process failures. To minimize such failures, maintenance must be a top priority.

This chapter stresses the importance of the maintenance process as a profit center and reviews the key requirements for supply chain maintenance success. It examines three of the maintenance best practices (reliability, preventive maintenance, and predictive maintenance) and presents an overview of planning for maintenance excellence.

25 Requirements for Effective Maintenance Leadership

When a Future Capable Company prepares for continuous improvement, it should include the evaluation and improvement of its current maintenance processes. There are a number of key principles and best practices that are fundamental to continuous improvement. Understanding the following 25 Requirements for Effective Maintenance Leadership should provide measurable benefits for the Future Capable Company's total operation.

1. View maintenance as a priority. The process of performing maintenance and managing physical assets should be a priority in the Future Capable Company. Maintenance should be viewed as another area that contributes directly to the bottom line when a strategy for continuous maintenance improvement is adopted. The Future Capable leader should understand best practices and should have identified priority areas for improvement based upon a total benchmark evaluation of the maintenance operation. Investments should be made to implement best practices.

2. Develop leadership and technical understanding. Maintenance leaders must understand the challenges of maintenance and provide effective maintenance leadership with a vision of continuous maintenance improvement. Maintenance leadership must continually develop the skills, abilities, and attitudes necessary to lead maintenance into the future. They should understand the 25 Requirements for Effective Maintenance Leadership and develop

priorities for action. In addition, they should foster understanding within the organization about maintenance and develop a vision of continuous maintenance improvement shared throughout the organization.

3. Develop PRIDE—People Really Interested in Developing Excellence in maintenance. Maintenance operations in the Future Capable Company should experience fundamental improvements in work ethics, attitude, values, job performance, and customer service to achieve real pride in maintenance excellence. Successful maintenance operations should have leadership that instills PRIDE and creates inspiration, cooperation, and commitment throughout the organization. Tangible savings and improvements should occur as a result of continuous maintenance improvement.

4. Recognize the importance of the maintenance profession. Maintenance should gain greater importance as the role of chief maintenance officer (CMO) becomes established during the early stages of the new millennium. Maintenance leaders should be recognized as critical resources necessary for the success of the total operation. The CMO in large multisite operations should create and promote standard best practices. The complexity and importance of maintenance and physical asset management will continue to grow because new technologies and added responsibilities will require more knowledge and skills.

5. Increase capability of maintenance personnel. A significant upgrade in the level of maintenance personnel should take place to keep pace with new technologies and responsibilities. Successful maintenance operations should continually upgrade the skill level of crafts people through effective recruiting with higher standards and through more effective craft-training programs. Pay increases should be more directly linked to performance and demonstrated competency levels in required craft skills.

6. Initiate craft skills development to enhance human capital. Successful maintenance operations should continually assess craft training needs and provide effective skills development through modern technical learning systems and competency based development of required skills. A complete assessment of craft training needs should be accomplished to identify priority areas for skill development. Skill development should be competency based to

provide demonstrated technical capabilities for each craft skill. The successful maintenance operation should develop an ongoing program for craft skill development. Continuous maintenance education based on modern technical learning systems should be viewed as a sound investment and an important part of continuous maintenance improvement.

7. Develop adaptability and versatility. The maintenance crafts work force should become more versatile and adaptable by gaining value with new technical capabilities and multicraft skills. The development of crafts people with multiple skills should occur to provide greater versatility, adaptability, and capability from the existing workforce. Multiskilled personnel should have added value. Crafts people should become more adaptable, versatile, and valuable as a result of ongoing programs for craft skill development.

8. Promote teamwork as a Future Capable Company strategy. Maintenance staff should be team players and maintain a leadership-driven, team-based approach to continuous maintenance improvement. Maintenance leadership should accept its role as a top-priority operation and should set the example as team players within the organization. The strategy for continuous maintenance improvement should be a leadership-driven, team-based approach that captures the knowledge, skills, and ideas of the entire maintenance work force. Cross-functional teams with representatives from maintenance, operations, and engineering should be formally chartered to address improvements to equipment effectiveness, reliability, and maintainability.

9. Establish effective maintenance planning and scheduling. Customer satisfaction and the utilization of available craft time should improve through more effective planning and scheduling systems. Developing better systems should be a top priority for the Future Capable maintenance operation. As reductions in breakdown repairs occur through effective preventive and/or predictive maintenance, the opportunity to increase planned maintenance work should result. Maintenance and operations should work closely to schedule repairs at the most convenient time. Maintenance should become more customer-oriented and focus on achieving greater customer satisfaction by completing sched-

uled repairs on time. The utilization of craft time should increase as levels of planned work increase and as the uncertainties and inefficiencies associated with breakdown repairs are reduced.

10. Maintenance and manufacturing operations should be a partnership for profits. Maintenance and manufacturing operations should become integrated and function as a supportive team through improved planning, scheduling, and cooperative, team-based improvement efforts. Operations should be viewed as an important internal customer. Improved planning and scheduling of maintenance work should provide greater coordination, support, and service to manufacturing-type operations. Maintenance and manufacturing operations of all types should recognize the benefits of working together as a supportive team to reduce unplanned breakdowns, to increase equipment effectiveness, and to reduce overall maintenance costs. Manufacturing should be viewed as an important internal customer and gain greater understanding of the 25 Requirements of Maintenance Leadership. It should also accept its important partnership role in supporting maintenance excellence.

11. Develop pride in ownership. Equipment operators and maintenance should develop a partnership for maintenance service and prevention and take greater pride in ownership through operator-based maintenance. Equipment operators should assume greater responsibilities for cleaning, lubricating, inspecting, monitoring, and making minor repairs to equipment. Maintenance should provide training support to operators to achieve this transfer of responsibility and help operators with early detection and prevention of maintenance problems. Operators should develop greater pride in ownership of their equipment with their expanded responsibilities.

12. Improve equipment effectiveness. Maintenance and manufacturing operations should use a leadership-driven, team-based approach to totally evaluate, and subsequently improve, all factors related to equipment effectiveness. The goal is to obtain maximum availability of the asset for performing its primary manufacturing function. Continually improving equipment effectiveness should address major losses due to equipment breakdowns, setup/adjustments, idling/minor stoppages, reduced speeds,

process defects, and reduced yields. Reliability Improvement Teams should be established to meet on a regular basis to identify and resolve equipment-related problems. They should work constructively as cross-functional teams to exchange and implement ideas for improving equipment effectiveness. They should use techniques such as Continuous Reliability Improvement (CRI) and Reliability Centered Maintenance (RCM). Chronic problems should be analyzed using tools such as statistical process control, graphs, process charts, and cause-and-effect analysis. Maintenance operations within successful Future Capable Companies should use a total team effort by operators, engineering, operations staff, and maintenance to identify and resolve root causes of equipment problems.

13. Maintenance and Engineering: A partnership for profitable technology application. Maintenance and engineering should work closely together during systems specification, installation, start-up, and operation to provide maintenance with the technical depth required for maintaining all assets and systems. Engineering should provide technical resources and support to ensure maintenance has the technical capability to maintain all equipment and systems. Engineering should support maintenance in improving the effectiveness of existing equipment. Maintenance and engineering should work closely together in developing specifications for new equipment. During installation and start-up, maintenance and engineering should also work closely together to ensure operating specifications are achieved.

14. Continuously improve reliability and maintainability. Machines and systems should be specified, designed, retrofitted, and installed with greater reliability and ease of maintainability. Equipment design should focus on maintainability and reliability, not just performance. Design for maintainability is an accepted philosophy that fully recognizes the high cost of maintenance in the life-cycle of equipment. High life-cycle costs can be reduced by applying good maintainability and reliability principles during design. Identify potential problems before they are designed into the equipment. Equipment design should include a higher level of internal diagnostic capabilities and provide greater use of expert systems for troubleshooting. Maintenance should work closely

with equipment designers to share information about problems with existing equipment. They should provide possible maintenance-prevention solutions during the design and/or specification process for new equipment.

15. Design for modularity. Physical assets and systems should be modularly designed so that failures are quickly identified and repaired. Overall maintainability should be further improved through modular design of physical assets and systems. Highest-failure parts and components should be the most accessible, easily identified, and designed for easy repair. Components should be designed for easy disassembly and reassembly using the lowest skill level possible. Modularity should be an important part of the design.

16. Manage life-cycle cost and obsolescence. The life-cycle costs of physical assets and systems should be closely monitored, evaluated, and managed to reduce total costs. During the equipment's operating life, systems should be developed to continually monitor equipment costs. Information should be available to highlight equipment with high-maintenance costs. A complete history of the equipment's repair costs should help maintenance in deciding on equipment replacement, overhaul/retrofit, and overall condition.

17. Create value-adding redundancy. Critical assets and systems should have backups so that if something fails, a secondary asset or system takes over. Critical operations and constraints to throughput should be identified. Redundancy of critical equipment and systems ensures continuous operation during failure. Maintenance should focus on critical operations to increase equipment effectiveness, reduce unplanned breakdowns, and increase the effectiveness of preventive/predictive maintenance.

18. Minimize uncertainty and eliminate root causes. Uncertainty should be minimized through effective preventive/predictive maintenance programs and through continuous application of modern predictive maintenance technology and expert systems. Effective preventive/predictive maintenance programs should be used to anticipate and predict problems to eliminate uncertainty of unexpected breakdowns and high repair costs. Predictive maintenance should not be limited solely to detecting failure but should proactively identify and eliminate the root causes of chronic

problems. Preventive/predictive maintenance programs should be adequately staffed to cover all major assets within the operation. Maintenance should maintain current technical knowledge and experience for applying a combination of predictive technologies best suited for the specific asset.

19. Maximize use of Computerized Maintenance Management and Enterprise Asset Management. Systems that support the total maintenance operation should improve the quality of maintenance and physical asset management and be integrated with the overall business system of the organization. Computerized Maintenance Management Systems (CMMS) should provide greater levels of manageability to maintenance operations. CMMS should cover the total scope of the maintenance operation and provide the means to improve the overall quality of maintenance management. Enterprise Asset Management (EAM) should provide a broader scope of integrated software to manage physical assets, human resources, and parts inventory in an integrated system for maintenance management, procurement, inventory management, work management, asset performance, and process monitoring. Vast amounts of data associated with maintenance tasks should be computer-controlled and available as key information for planning, scheduling, backlog control, equipment history, parts availability, inventory control, performance measurement, and downtime analysis.

20. Use maintenance information to manage the business of maintenance. The maintenance information system and database should encompass the total maintenance function and provide real-time information to improve maintenance management. Implementing CMMS and EAM provides the opportunity for improved maintenance information systems. With CMMS and EAM, the maintenance information system can be developed and tailored to support maintenance as a true "business operation." Information to support planning, scheduling, equipment history, preventive/predictive maintenance, and storeroom management can be established to improve decision-making and overall maintenance management. Improved maintenance information should allow for open communication between all departments within the organization. It is important that maintenance become an

integral part of the overall information flow and be kept well-informed about current and future operational plans.

21. Ensure an effective maintenance storeroom operation. The storeroom for Maintenance Repair Operations (MRO) should be orderly, space- and labor-efficient, responsive, and should encourage maintenance excellence. Initial storeroom design or modernization should provide a layout that ensures efficient inventory control and includes maximum loss-control measures. It should be professionally managed and maintained. The trend should be toward larger, centralized storerooms with responsive delivery systems to eliminate crafts people waiting or traveling to get parts. An effective maintenance storeroom catalog should be maintained to provide a permanent cross-reference of all storeroom items and to serve as a tool for identifying and locating items.

22. Establish the spare parts inventory as the cornerstone for effective maintenance. The proper quantity of spare parts should be on hand, as a part of progressive MRO procurement and internal storeroom controls, to support maintenance excellence. The implementation of CMMS and EAM should include an inventory system that supports the requirements of maintenance and the storeroom. Maintenance inventory should be managed to ensure that the right part is available at the right time without excessive inventory levels. Information from all available sources should be used to determine optimum stock levels. Continuously review stock levels to eliminate excess inventory and obsolete parts. Inventory reductions should be achieved through more partnerships with suppliers and vendors who establish joint commitments to purchase based on responsive service and fast delivery. Positions within MRO material management and procurement should increase in their importance and level of technical knowledge to perform effectively.

23. Establish a safe and productive working environment. Successful maintenance operations should be safe, clean, and orderly because good housekeeping is an indicator of maintenance excellence. Maintenance leaders should provide a working environment where safety is a top priority. This, in turn, sets an example throughout the organization. Good housekeeping practices in maintenance

provide the basic foundation for safety awareness. Maintenance should provide support throughout the organization to ensure that all work areas are safe, clean, and orderly.

24. Aggressively support compliance with environmental, health, and safety requirements. Maintenance must provide proactive leadership for and support of regulatory compliance actions in the Future Capable Company. U.S.-based maintenance leaders must maintain the technical knowledge and experience to support compliance with all state and federal regulations under OSHA, USEPA, FDA, the U.S. Department of Transportation, and the Americans with Disabilities Act. Non-U.S.-based companies and American businesses operating abroad must comply with all standards of the nation they are operating. Indoor air quality must receive constant attention to eliminate potential problems. Maintenance must work closely with quality and safety and other groups to provide a totally integrated and mutually supportive approach to regulatory compliance.

25. Continuously evaluate, measure, and improve maintenance performance and service. Broad-based measures of maintenance performance and customer service should provide a continuous evaluation of the maintenance program. CMMS and EAM should allow for a broad range of measurement for maintenance performance and service. Investment in maintenance best practices should ensure a valid return on investment. Projected savings should be established, and the results should be validated. Measures should be developed in areas such as labor performance/utilization, compliance to planned repair, and preventive/predictive maintenance schedules, current backlog levels, emergency repair hours, storeroom performance, and asset uptime and availability. Leaders of successful maintenance operations should continuously evaluate performance and service to manage maintenance as a business.

The 25 Requirements for Effective Maintenance Leadership provide the foundation for developing maintenance excellence. An effective maintenance process is essential to the Future Capable Company. It all starts with a total commitment to a strategy of continuous maintenance improvement, with maintenance as a top priority. That means realizing that maintenance is a key contributor to an organization's profit and that maintenance best practices, plus people, plus MRO assets, plus information technology all combine for the success and improvement of the total maintenance operation.

RELIABILITY

Reliability means focusing on how to improve maintainability and reliability, not on asset performance. This can be accomplished by applying RCM and CRI. The key elements of RCM include:

- Analyzing and deciding what must be done to ensure excellent performance
- Defining the users' expectations for primary performance parameters such as output, throughput, speed, range, and carrying capacity
- Defining what users want in terms of risk, process and operational safety, environmental integrity, quality of output, control, comfort, economy of operation, and customer satisfaction
- Identifying the state of failures, ways that assets can fail, and the consequences of those failures
- Conducting Failure Modes and Effects Analysis (FMEA) to identify all the events likely to cause each failed state
- Identifying a suitable reliability management policy for dealing with each failure mode in light of its consequences

CRI goes well beyond the traditional approaches found in RCM, which focuses primarily on the physical asset. CRI is a total maintenance improvement process that supports the Future Capable Company. To focus the team processes on continuous reliability improvement opportunities, CRI considers the following:

- Physical asset: Use of reliability improvement technologies; reliability-centered maintenance, preventive/predictive maintenance, and knowledge-based expert systems for maintenance of the physical asset. Asset facilitation is used to gain maximum capacity at the lowest possible life-cycle cost.
- MRO material resources: Effective MRO parts, supplies, and materials for quality repair with effective storeroom operations and procurement processes.
- Information resources: Quality information resources for maintenance management and control from CMMS, EAM, ERP,

vendor, and customer.

- Craft resources: Quality craft skill improvements for the people who support customer satisfaction throughout the Future Capable Company.
- Operator resources: The added value of equipment operators instilled with pride in ownership to support maintenance at the most important level—the manufacturing shop floor.
- Synergistic team processes: Leadership-driven groups providing effective teaming that multiplies people assets.

The goal of reliability is not only to reduce failure rates, but also to eliminate root causes of failure. This means identifying a suitable reliability improvement policy that includes two of today's best practices: predictive maintenance and preventive maintenance. The difference between preventive and predictive maintenance is simply the differences between an interval-based system (preventive maintenance) and a condition-based system (predictive maintenance). Management has two basic choices for a maintenance repair strategy:

1. Run to Failure. Continue to operate with a high level of uncertainty by running equipment or operating facilities at required capacity and shutting down only for emergency repairs. Continue to gamble with the costs of maintenance and unexpected downtime.

2. Planned Maintenance with Preventive Maintenance. Reduce the uncertainty of unplanned downtime and emergency repairs with a program of planned inspections, adjustments, lubrications, and testing/monitoring with predictive maintenance tools and techniques.

PREVENTIVE MAINTENANCE (PM)— AN INTERVAL-BASED SYSTEM

PM is an interval-based surveillance method in which periodic inspections are performed on equipment to determine the wear on components and sub-systems. When wear has advanced to a degree that warrants correction, maintenance is performed on the asset. The corrective maintenance can be performed at the time of the inspection or later as part of planned maintenance. The decision depends on the length of shutdown required for the repair.

Consider the impact of shutting down the operation for the repair vs. how immediate the need is for repair. If the worn component allows the asset to operate without major damage, then repairs may be postponed until they can be planned and scheduled. A PM system increases the probability that the equipment should perform as expected without failure until the next inspection.

Determining the interval between inspections requires considering the history of maintenance for the equipment in each unique operation. Ultimately, intervals between PM inspections should be guided by a number of resources. These include manufacturer's recommendations, feedback information from repair history of breakdowns, and the subjective knowledge of the maintenance crafts people and supervisors who maintain the asset on a daily basis. Equipment operators may also be a good source of information in some operations.

A central characteristic of preventive maintenance is that in most major applications, the asset must be shut down for inspection. The inspection process requires a discrete amount of downtime for the asset. The loss of operational time when significant preventive maintenance inspections are made is one of the reasons PM programs are often less than successful. This is especially true in applications where there are few redundant units and equipment must operate at 100 percent of capacity. In some situations the loss from shutdown is considered too high a penalty, and preventive maintenance inspections are resisted. The truth is, that preventive maintenance, when properly applied, unquestionably increases overall equipment availability and is a key contributor to improved reliability.

PREDICTIVE MAINTENANCE (PdM)— A CONDITION-BASED SYSTEM

In contrast to preventive maintenance, predictive maintenance is a condition-based system. PdM measures some output from equipment that is related to the degeneration of the asset, a component, or subsystem. For example, vibration analysis equipment might measure metal fatigue on the face of a rolling element bearing. As deterioration progresses, the amplitude of vibration increases. At some critical value, the vibration analyzer concludes that corrective action should be taken to avoid catastrophic failure.

Predictive maintenance usually permits discrete measurements, which may be compared with some predefined limit (baseline) or tracked using statistical control charting. When an anomaly is observed, warning is provided in sufficient time to analyze the nature of the problem and take corrective action to avoid failure. Thus, predictive maintenance contributes to the same central objective for increased reliability. With early detection of wear, you can plan for and take corrective action to retard the rate of wear, prevent or minimize the impact of failure, and predict failure. The corrective maintenance restores the component or sub-assembly, and the asset operates with a greater probability of trouble-free performance.

The enhanced ability to trend and plot numbers collected from PdM measurements gives this method greater sensitivity than traditional preventive maintenance methods. The technique yields earlier warning of severe wear and thus provides greater lead-time for maintenance to react. Corrective actions may be scheduled so that they have minimum impact on operations.

A principal advantage of predictive maintenance is the capability it offers the user to perform inspections while the equipment is operating. In fact, in order to reflect routine operating conditions, the technique requires taking measurements when the equipment is normally loaded in its production environment. Since the machine does not need to be removed from the production cycle, there is no shutdown penalty.

The nature of the operation should determine which methods are most effective. In practice, it takes some combination of preventive and PdM to assure maximum reliability. How much of each should vary with the type of equipment and the percent of the time these machines are operating. When comparing the cost advantages of PdM over PM, consider production downtime costs, maintenance labor costs, maintenance materials costs, and the cost of holding spare parts in inventory.

PLANNING FOR MAINTENANCE EXCELLENCE

Planning for maintenance excellence requires planning at both the strategic level and at the shop-floor level. Without effective planning and scheduling, maintenance operations continue to operate in a reactive, fire-fighting mode that wastes their most valuable resource—craft time. Gambling with maintenance costs is not an option for Future Capable Companies. A world-class operation requires a world-class maintenance program. Effective planning and scheduling of valuable craft skills and labor resources is an essential best practice in the Future Capable Company's plan of action.

The ultimate success of maintenance planning and scheduling should be determined by whether or not the customer is satisfied. All preliminary work to develop a plan and to coordinate the scheduled repairs is wasted if execution of the schedule does not occur. The customer (operations) should determine the true success of the planning process. The entire maintenance workforce must understand how they serve operations. As a formal planning process is implemented, an increased focus on customer satisfaction must be established. Operations should expect improved satisfaction, and maintenance must commit to providing it.

Effective planning and scheduling also requires that reasonable estimates and planning times be established for as much maintenance work as possible. Planning times provide a number of benefits for the planning function. They provide a means to determine existing workloads for scheduling by craft areas and the backlog of work in each area. They allow the maintenance planner to balance repair priorities against available craft hours and to realistically establish repair schedules that can be accomplished as promised. Planning times also provide a target for each planned job, and that, in turn, allows for craft performance measurement.

With an understanding of best practices such as reliability, preventive and predictive maintenance, and maintenance planning, the CEO or CMO of a Future Capable Company should be well equipped for the future. Application of the 25 Requirements for Maintenance Leadership and implementation of the following six-step plan of action should ensure success of maintenance and the total operation:

• Evaluate the current state of maintenance
• Determine strengths and weaknesses
• Determine potential results from improvement opportunities
• Develop and implement a strategic maintenance plan
• Validate results and return on investment
• Continually improve reliability

SUMMARY AND CALL TO ACTION

The Future Capable Company has a firm understanding of the physical asset management and maintenance process and its important role. It recognizes the contribution of maintenance to Total Operations' success and profitability. Effective maintenance and physical asset management are closely linked to enterprise-wide performance success and profitability.

The 25 Requirements for Maintenance Leadership provide the foundation for the maintenance strategy, which is part of overall business planning. Today's best maintenance practices are being used within Future Capable Companies. The results of continuous maintenance improvement are being measured, and the results and ROI are being continuously validated.

Maintenance is forever. To meet the Maintenance Requirements of Success, the Future Capable Company must recognize that maintenance is a key contributor to total supply chain success.

chapter 13

HUMAN CAPITAL

F uture Capable Companies must view employees as their most
important assets because without their commitment, continuous
improvement will not happen. Organizations must value intellectual capital and secure their growth by making sure all
employees are satisfied, happy, and challenged.

"Employees are a company's most valuable asset." How
often does that appear in company memos or framed
prints in an organization's hallway? Although it may seem
it's said so often that it has lost its value, in reality it's not
said enough. It is a philosophy that tends to be lost
among profit and loss margins, and it should not be.
When a company begins viewing its employees as assets,
then that company can begin to maximize their participation in its operations and its successes. An effective means
of maximizing their participation is to realize the value of
their intellectual capital. Knowledge is such a prized com-
modity in today's marketplace that many workers are now
being called "knowledge workers." Companies that use
this capital to their advantage, while also making sure that
their employees have been provided with the tools they
need to grow and succeed, are Future Capable Companies.

Future Capable Companies view employees as their
most important assets, knowing that without them, continuous improvement will not be achieved. Therefore, they
invest in their employees. They also create an environment
where every employee is motivated and happy, so these
companies make the most of those investments.

To create this environment, the Future Capable Company fosters:
• Future Capable Leadership
• Cultural revolution
• Development
• Trust

This chapter discusses these elements of human capital, demonstrating how to value intellectual capital and secure its growth by making sure all employees are satisfied, happy, and challenged.

FUTURE CAPABLE LEADERSHIP

Energetic, passionate, intense, and determined people characterize Future Capable Companies. Therefore, they need leaders who are even more energetic, passionate, intense, and determined than they are. They need Future Capable Leaders.

Future Capable Leaders have these qualities:
• Integrity—Future Capable Leaders live and tell the truth, deal with people and situations in a straightforward, sincere fashion, and behave ethically.
• Credibility—Future Capable Leaders are accountable, genuine, and open.
• Enthusiasm—Future Capable Leaders show their excitement about the future, because such excitement is contagious.
• Optimism—Future Capable Leaders are confident about what they are doing to focus on success.
• Urgency—GO, GO, GO! Future Capable Leaders know that the only way to affect the future is to act now. They do not spend a great deal of time savoring their successes, because they are already focusing on the future.
• Determination—Future Capable Leaders step forward to face doubts and uncertainties, to accept risk, to move forward, and to make real their understanding that there are no boundaries between their organizations and gaining competitive advantage. Relying on these characteristics, Future Capable Leaders motivate others by the way they communicate, work, and treat others. Future Capable Leaders recognize the importance of effective communication, and they arm people with certainty and control through direct communication and sharing information. They seek out other Future

Capable Leaders in their supply chain partnerships and share skills and knowledge.

Future Capable Leaders motivate others by the way they work, because they adhere to personal work policies that result in working hard and smart. These policies are:

- Make the right decision, adhering to the "three rights": the right decisions at the right time communicated to the right people.
- Focus on process management, not time management, and prepare for interruptions. Interruptions can provide a much-needed picture of what may really be happening with a project or projects.
- Pay attention to the right details. Delegate those details that are not relevant to the decision at hand to others who are capable of handling them.
- Go the extra mile by exceeding all expectations, particularly in the areas of friendliness, responsiveness, and attentiveness. Finally, Future Capable Leaders treat others in the way others want to be treated.
- Realize that change is inevitable and accept, anticipate, and harness it, while realizing that mistakes are not only possible, they are inevitable, and must be admitted.

FUTURE CAPABLE LEADERSHIP: THE WORLD'S MOST ADMIRED COMPANIES

Every quarter, BP Amoco maps the progress of its "people." It targets qualitative performance measures such as innovation, mutual trust and respect, teamwork, and diversity. Like many of the companies on Fortune Magazine's Global Most Admired list, BP Amoco recognizes that achievements in these areas are just as important to the success of the company as revenues, profits, and other financial measures. To separate the Global Most Admired from their competition, the Hay Group surveyed these companies and their peers about the performance measures they use to chart the progress of their companies.

Senior executives in the Most Admired Companies

Continued

FUTURE CAPABLE LEADERSHIP *Continued from page 137*

believe that their performance measures encourage cooperation and collaboration. They reported that such measures help their companies focus on growth, operational excellence, customer loyalty, human capital development, and other critical issues. "The companies on the Most Admired list have chief executives who understand what performance measurement is all about," says Hay Group Managing Director Vicky Wright. "It's not about keeping score. It's about learning how to motivate people—how to link those performance measures with real rewards." Given their enthusiasm for performance measurements, it was not surprising to learn that leaders in Most Admired Companies were more involved in the goal-setting process than their counterparts. More than 90 percent of CEOs participated in goal setting at the Most Admired Companies, compared with 71 percent at other companies.

The findings confirm the importance of considering the financial and human aspects of performance and linking them to short- and long-term incentives. "The top organizations create performance measures that focus on all the drivers of their businesses—financial performance, shareholder value, employees, and customers," says Hay Group Vice President William Alper. "They involve their boards and top leaders in the process, and they link the results directly to executive incentives."

–Fortune, October 2, 2000

Future Capable Leaders treat people in the way those people want to be treated. They offer compassion, politeness, trust, dignity, respect, and fairness. In doing so, they motivate people, because people who are treated as they wish to be treated are more likely to offer the same courtesies to others.

Through their actions, Future Capable Leaders foster the environment necessary for investing in the human capital required to create a Future Capable Company. They are aware of how important employees are and how much value they add to an organization. They lead and participate in the cultural revolution that creates the Future Capable Company.

CULTURAL REVOLUTION

Culture is the foundation for an organization. It permeates every organizational activity and event. Each organization has a unique culture that plays a part in its success. The Future Capable Company is no exception.

A Future Capable Company cultural revolution occurs through the ongoing transformation of rules, habits, procedures, standards, norms, rewards, language, stories, expectations, ceremonies, and titles—in short, all the elements that affect employee screening and retention, cultural evolution, organizational behavior, and, finally, organizational performance. At odds with this transformation is the organization's existing culture, which will try to stifle a new one. Therefore, a cultural revolution is not a number of simple changes, but instead it is an across-the-board ongoing transformation that wears away at traditional manifestations and perceptions until they no longer exist.

This transformation begins with the evolution of the organization's direction. A Future Capable Leader continuously refines the new path for his or her organization. He or she continuously responds to the business environment, adjusts the path, and shines a light on the new path while communicating a sense of urgency. The Future Capable Leader stretches, pushes, and pulls the Future Capable Company culture into the future. He or she replaces today's solution with tomorrow's and the solution after next.

For a cultural revolution to be successful, an evolution of understanding the new path for each employee is critical and will help dissipate organizational resistance. As I mentioned earlier, Future Capable Leaders motivate people through communication, their work behavior, and how they treat others. Through open, honest, credible, enthusiastic, and respectful communication and behavior, Future Capable Leaders can make serious inroads into dissipating organizational resistance.

A cultural revolution can also be held back by fear of the unknown. Fear is often the cause of resistance, because most people fear change, and a cultural revolution means changes—big ones. An organizational culture can combat fear in several ways. One is through reassurance that the good things promised employees as a result of the revolution really will happen. This reassurance takes time, because plans often have to be in place before their benefits can be perceived. The Future Capable Leader uses re-recruitment to accomplish this reassurance and ensure enthusiasm and support for the organization's cultural revolution.

A combination of education and training, known as development, also combats fear. Development creates knowledgeable, confident employees who can work both hard and smart while enjoying their work. These employees can identify problems and offer solutions— another key ingredient in the Future Capable Company recipe.

The concept of re-recruitment came to me while sitting on the board of directors of a very successful electronics distribution company. At a particular board meeting with management, executive management, and the board present, the HR manager was explaining the company's new procedures on recruiting. These procedures included:
- Limo service for airport pickup
- Four-star hotel instead of motel
- Breakfast with executive management
- Flowers sent to a spouse while the mate was being interviewed
    As I listened to this explanation I noted:
- The Board was pleased to hear of new procedures.
- Executive management already understood the new procedures and nodded their heads.
- Management had an attitude of, "Wow, what about me? I took a cab to a motel, ate breakfast by myself, and my spouse got nothing."

It hit me, that, yes, recruitment was important, but even more important was the continuous improvement of the "employee deal," the continuous re-recruitment of our people to ensure our long-term success.

Re-recruitment involves improving the work conditions, benefits, culture, and perks offered to all onboard employees. Re-recruitment results in higher loyalty, retention, and an essence of inclusion.

Re-recruitment involves the following:
- Challenging long-held policies. Policies surrounding work arrangements should not be based on historical precedent. Instead, they

should emphasize whether those arrangements will enhance or hinder the organization's ability to retain good performers in the future. For example, a company that refuses to allow part-time work arrangements forces an ultimatum upon employees whose life may now require part-time work. Both the employee and the enterprise lose.

- Re-examining established procedures. In one fast-growing company, the executive vice president responsible for e-business needed to quickly build staff. Rather than look among new, untried applicants, the vice president decided to search for former high-performing employees and invite them to rejoin the company. However, an attempt to gather the names and specialties of the former employees resulted in a roadblock. The company had neither the HR processes nor the incentive to identify and re-recruit those employees.

- Communicating corporate strategy and involving employees in decision-making. This builds loyalty and aids retention.

- Anticipating and preventing workforce departures. Because of today's mobile workforce, organization leaders should identify key people and define practices that will encourage them to remain with the organization. For both employers and employees, that means retaining strong and amicable ties with one another.

Throughout the cultural evolution process and during re-recruitment, the Future Capable Leader must keep one critical piece of information in mind: A Gallup poll, conducted over 25 years, recently revealed that the most important variable in employee productivity and loyalty is the relationship between employees and their supervisors.

The employees stated their supervisors could achieve this good relationship by doing the following:

- Setting clear and consistent expectations
- Caring for them
- Valuing their unique qualities
- Encouraging and supporting their growth and development

In other words, perks, benefits, and pay did not rate as high as the quality of supervision. A Future Capable Leader realizes that people leave managers, not companies, and works to ensure employees' internal and emotional satisfaction because that will gain the organization greater productivity and diminish fear, doubt, and uncertainty.

THE "Q12"

The Gallup Organization's Marcus Buckingham and Curt Coffman created a metric that clearly defines the bottom-line value of eliciting certain feelings from employees in the workplace. They can also predict how employees will perform by asking them 12 questions, which they call the "Q12." These questions are:

- Do I know what is expected of me at work?
- Do I have the materials and equipment I need to do my work right?
- At work, do I have the opportunity to do what I do best every day?
- In the last seven days, have I received recognition or praise for doing good work?
- Does my supervisor, or someone at work, seem to care about me as a person?
- Is there someone at work who encourages my development?
- At work, do my opinions seem to count?
- Does the mission/purpose of my company make me feel my job is important?
- Are my co-workers committed to doing quality work?
- Do I have a best friend at work?
- In the last six months, has someone at work talked to me about my progress?
- This past year, have I had opportunities at work to learn and grow?

Employees who answered "strongly agree" were 50 percent more likely to work in business units with lower employee turnover, 38 percent more likely to work in more productive business units, and 56 percent more likely to work in business units with high customer loyalty.

DEVELOPMENT

A development program that will maintain Future Capable employees, and thus result in a Future Capable Company, must first address the development needed. All employees need three types of development:

visionary development, general development, and specific development.

Visionary development is the basic foundation upon which happy and motivated employees evolve. This foundation was called basic beliefs, the bedrocks, philosophies of business, and Requirements of Success in Chapter 3. Visionary development is the consistency portion of dynamic consistency.

All employees involved in a supply chain, from CEOs to operations managers to document technicians, must understand the processes that create Future Capable Companies or there will be no shared beliefs and no Future Capable Employees or Future Capable Leaders. Therefore, the most important developmental need of every organization is for everyone in the company to understand the concept of the Future Capable Company. Fulfilling this visionary development need will be a major step toward becoming a Future Capable Company.

General developmental needs are categorized as general knowledge development and general skills development. General knowledge development includes an understanding of the following:

- How a company is organized
- The technology involved
- How products are used
- Who uses the products
- The company supply chain's competition
- The company's strengths, weaknesses, opportunities, and challenges

General skill development is learning skills that are needed to best contribute to a company's success. They include the following:

- Problem solving
- Planning
- Cost reduction
- Quality enhancement
- Communications
- Managing
- Goal setting
- Creativity
- Information technology and computer literacy

The challenge of general development is in determining who would benefit from which type. Typically, managers underestimate the value of having their employees exposed to general development. As a guideline, any developmental program of interest to a manager is probably also of interest to the manager's staff. Keep in mind that greater understanding leads to motivation and happiness.

Specific developmental needs are programs designed for special groups of individuals. For example, network administrators will require a specific program when a new system is installed; maintenance will require one when a new machine is installed; marketing and sales will require a specific developmental program when a new product is introduced.

Avoid overly restricting the participants in the specific developmental activities. Developing employees beyond their present position will provide the benefits of multiskilling discussed in Chapter 9.

Address how to achieve the development needed. The basic approach to developing is to uncover, discover, and recover. The first step, uncover, means that the need must be uncovered in the mind of the person being developed. This person must believe there is a purpose in developing new knowledge or skills. Next, there must be a discovery on the part of the participant of the new knowledge or skill. The person being developed must be immersed to the point where the brain comprehends the new knowledge or skill. Lastly, during recovery, the knowledge or skill is put into practice. Only by experimenting with the knowledge or skill is the development successful. Without recovery, there is no application of the knowledge or skill, and thus, no true development.

Each company should establish a development program that meets the needs of the employees, then continually evolve these programs. A good development program should adhere to some basic development principles:

- Development must be done just-in-time: Uncover the need for knowledge, discover new knowledge, and recover by putting new knowledge into action.
- Development must be part of the process of creating Peak-to-Peak Performance and, therefore, aligned with the Future Capable Company's vision, using the link's teaming vocabulary, culture, and process.
- Development must be flexible. In other words, individual needs must be assessed and the development program customized to meet them.

- Development must have full leadership support at all levels. This support should be proactive.
- Development must be presented in short, interactive sessions by high-quality, well-prepared, and interesting people.
- Development must be built into the schedule so that people are not behind on their functions after they return from a development session.
- Development must be accountable. It is important to conduct follow-up tests, probes, and measurements to determine the development's effectiveness. Employees should be recognized for successfully completing a development program or session.
- Teams should be the focus of development.
- Development must be viewed as a priority.
- Development objectives must be focused. The facilitator and all development session attendees must understand what they will learn from the training, and they must then be able to state why it is important to them.
- Development programs do not have to be sessions conducted in a classroom. There are a number of other development methods that follow the principles above.

    Some examples include the following:
- Computer-based development—CD ROMS and other interactive learning.
- Web-based development—development programs and classes available on the World Wide Web. These are sponsored by companies, individuals, and even universities.
- Virtual universities—Web-based university classes that combine Web-based, interactive classes with video-conferencing and "chat" via the Web.
- Planning retreats—off-site, multiday planning meetings for upper management to evaluate progress and develop strategic plans.
- Employee retreats—off-site, multiday meetings for a broad cross section of employees in which the vision for the company and strategic plans are presented and goals and objectives are established.
- Planning forums—on-site, half-day meetings for upper management to review progress and adjust strategic plans.
- Staff meetings—on-site, half-day updates for all employees on com-

pany progress and general development topics.

- Communications meetings—on-site, two-hour meetings on company status.
- New employee orientation—a multiweek process involving meeting with other employees, reading materials, watching video tapes, and following computer-based or Web-based training courses to obtain an understanding of the vision of the company and the general development required to be productive.
- Seminars—multiday, single-speaker presentations addressing specific development topics.
- Trade shows—multiday shows where specific development will result from interacting one-on-one with people who have experiences relevant to company needs.
- Plant tours—visits to plants to obtain specific development on systems applications.
- Professional society meetings—meetings containing a brief presentation on general interest topics.
- Trade and professional journals—a variety of publications addressing every manufacturing theme and aspect.
- Books—both general-interest and specific-interest books that provide in-depth coverage of a topic.
- Videos—tapes that illustrate and demonstrate the functions and application of equipment and systems.
- Equipment files/databases—well-maintained files and databases on vendor equipment and systems literature.
- Topic files/databases—intranet files and databases containing articles, proceedings, and speeches on specific topics of interest.
- Industry files/databases—files and databases containing clipped information on companies and industries that are marketing targets.
- Competition files/databases—files and databases containing literature and background information on all competition.
- Client files/databases—a file or database of all past clients and all past equipment/systems applications containing proposals, reports, and supporting materials documenting past client interactions. A reference should direct users to the appropriate client files for information.
- Equipment cost guides—A computerized guide to allow costing out of alternative equipment and systems.

- In-house development—specific development meetings where new software or technical methodologies are presented and illustrated.
- On-the-job development—the utilization by a senior person of a real project to develop a less-experienced person on project technology and methodology.

Future Capable Companies understand that development must be flexible to meet the needs and learning styles of their employees. They encourage development because it is one of the best ways for them to alleviate the fears perpetrated by a resistant, existing culture and, at the same time, earn trust.

TRUST

Hiring a Future Capable Employee and providing for the person's development is not enough to keep him or her motivated and happy. There must also be trust. Without trust:

- There are no motivated and happy employees.
- There is no respect, and thus, no loyalty.
- There is no participation and no success.
- There is no Future Capable Company.

When trust exists, employees and managers respect each other. From respect comes a sincere desire to listen, which results in an understanding of the other's perspective. Understanding results in a concern for another's well-being; concern grows into a collaborative style that allows management and employees to openly discuss goals and directions. This leads to success, which gives way to positive reinforcement that makes employees happy and motivates them to work for further positive reinforcement. This is winning. The result is a Future Capable Company. Leaders, managers, and employees establish a range of healthy communication that results in continuous winning. It all occurs because, up front, there was trust.

Some companies have pursued a whole legacy of programs to attempt to obtain employee participation. In companies where trust exists, these programs work very well. However, without trust, these concepts become fads about which the employees will moan and think, "This too shall pass." The issue is not which program is applied. The issue is one of basic trust. If there is no trust, there is no winning.

Some may take exception to my use of the term employees in this book. Some prefer to call employees partners, associates, stakeholders, or members. There is nothing wrong with these terms, but without trust, the terminology is of little importance. In fact, if there is trust, there is no problem with the term employees. All the management books, the discussions on employee involvement and participation, and the fixation with other organizations' "magic" successes really boil down to achieving a mutual trust between management and employees. Only when every manager is dedicated to hiring, developing, and trusting winners will employees be motivated and happy. Only then will companies win. And winning companies are Future Capable Companies.

HOW TO MAXIMIZE HUMAN CAPITAL

Maximizing human capital requires a long-term, consistent effort. It also includes:

- A lasting commitment to employees
- The confidence of all employees in this commitment
- The development of all employees
- A mutual trust among all employees
- The cooperation and teamwork of all employees

There are no short cuts or easy solutions. Only by pursuing the processes of Future Capable Leadership, cultural revolution, development, and trust will a company maximize human capital and create a Future Capable Company.

CONTINUOUS
IMPROVEMENT

ith the pace of Change and the rate of innovation, what is a great process today will be suspect in a few months and obsolete shortly thereafter. The Future Capable Company must be aware of this and continually evaluate, analyze, and improve its processes.

To many people, success is the ultimate goal. Unfortunately, success is rarely final. The natural order of life is peak-to-valley-to-peak-to-valley, and so on. This starts with the thrill of the climb to the peak of entrepreneurship. The peak represents success. However, after the success comes the need to protect the peak, and the entrepreneurial spirit is soon mired down in management, budgets, and standard operating procedures. The company soon tumbles off the peak into a valley, which represents failure. Some companies never return from the valley; others climb back up with renewed creativity and spirit only to slide back down under the reins of management's need to be protective.

As the founder, chairman, and president of a Total Operations consulting, systems implementation, and material handling integration firm, I have taken my organization on the peak-to-valley journey. Through my experience at the top of peaks and at the bottom of valleys, I have determined the following four evolutions of a company:

1   Fail/fail
2. Fail/succeed
3. Succeed/fail
4. Succeed/succeed

Fail/fail is usually a vicious cycle that keeps destroying confidence until the ultimate failure occurs. What puts companies in a fail/fail cycle? They do not learn from their mistakes. As the saying goes, "Insanity is doing the same thing over and over and expecting different results." There are many companies like this. You do not hear much about them because they never succeed. Or you hear that someone has bought them out before they went anywhere. Often these companies are led by CEOs who will not admit they make mistakes and run around blaming others in the company for their failures. Such companies quickly enter the fail/fail cycle.

Fail/succeed is the pattern of learning from mistakes to overcome setbacks. An example is a company whose CEO, after suffering a few failures, examines those failures, sees the good in them and recognizes the bad, and then begins working with management teams to eliminate the bad. Those who view failure as a challenge can turn adversity into the motivation to succeed.

Succeed/fail is the most common progression for many companies. The brief history of several B2C dot-coms is a good example of succeed/fail. After beginning with a surge of entrepreneurial energy, grabbing a lot of initial attention, making some big sales, and offering the latest e-commerce technology, many of them are gone after only a few years. There are many brick-and-mortars that follow the same pattern, though—large, easily recognized companies from almost every industry: automotive, retail, publishing, printing, pharmaceutical, and healthcare.

Succeed/succeed is the ultimate evolution. Companies that learn the formula for succeed/succeed to take the lead and hold on to it. They play to win instead of trying to avoid losing. They are Future Capable Companies. The key is Continuous Improvement. Companies that practice Continuous Improvement will put themselves in the succeed/succeed cycle.

The cornerstone of Continuous Improvement is collaboration through teamwork and partnerships. This chapter examines teamwork and partnerships within the framework of collaboration and outlines the steps necessary to practice Continuous Improvement and maintain a succeed/succeed cycle.

TEAMWORK AND PARTNERSHIP

To practice Continuous Improvement, an organization must understand collaboration and cooperation—with suppliers, within organizations, and with customers. Otherwise, there is no Future Capable Company. Within the organization, that's called teamwork; within the supply chain, it's called partnership.

Although many people throughout the organizations in a supply chain pay lip service to partnership, partnering is rarely truly practiced. Similarly, many organizations believe that calling a department a team is all that creating teamwork requires. Within these partnerships (teams), there are selfish, uncooperative organizations (people) who believe that someone can win only when someone else loses. The focus is on one-upmanship, petty politics, and dishonesty.

I could fill this book describing vendors who were victimized, internal politics that led to counterproductive activities, and customers who were not properly treated. But I'd rather discuss how to create the right kinds of teamwork and partnership. This requires following these guiding principles:

- All organizational units and supply chain links must be 100 percent directed toward the success of the whole supply chain.
- There can be no adversarial relationships within the organization or the supply chain.
- All organizational units must function as a cohesive, collective whole.
- An environment where every employee is motivated and happy will eliminate the we-vs.-they problem that undermines teamwork. In a Future Capable Company, there are no we-vs.-they relationships. There are only team players and partnerships.

TEAMING

The process used to develop Future Capable Company teams is:
1. Identify a leader
2. Identify team players

3. Specify the characteristics of a successful team
4. Establish cooperation
5. Establish a plan
6. Obtain success
7. Build on success
8. Return to Step 4

Let us take a closer look at these steps.

Identify a Leader and Team Players

Selecting a team leader is critical because the team will ultimately reflect the leader's beliefs. Identifying team players is equally important. No amount of coaching, managing, or leading can create a team if the players are not committed. An important question that must be asked early in the team-building process is, "Do we have the right players?" The right players must meet three criteria:

1. They must want to be a part of the team.
2. They must have the abilities the team requires.
3. They must be truly committed to the success of the team.

Specify the Characteristics of a Successful Team

All team members must understand the characteristics of a successful team because these characteristics serve as the criteria for determining team development. For Winning Manufacturing, the characteristics of a successful team are:

- Shared vision—All team players have a consistent vision of where the team is headed.
- Shared values—All team players adopt and adhere to a level of business ethics and honesty beyond levels that have been traditionally viewed as the norm. A code of ethics is not a book of do's and don'ts, but is the moral fiber of the team players. High ethical standards may result in the loss of some short-term opportunities, but in the long run, they will provide a basis for teamwork and trust.
- Shared expectations—There are no surprises for team players. The team has well-defined and understood expectations that are shared by all team players and serve as the basis for teamwork.
- Shared commitment—There is no such thing as a part-time team player. Team players are committed to the team and dedicated to mutual success and cooperation.

- Shared confidence—Each team player has confidence in all other team players.
- Shared responsibility—Communications, involvement, and interactions are frequent. Team players share responsibility for success and failure. Team players are accountable for their efforts and for the team's performance.
- Shared rewards—All team players benefit from the team's success.

Establish Cooperation

Having meetings or writing memos does not create cooperation; it requires joint participation on a Continuous Improvement project. During the project, the team must operate as a whole unit, and that's where cooperation comes in. By cooperating, team commitment and confidence grow, and there is a sense of team excellence. Conflict is viewed as an opportunity to learn. There is no win/lose mentality, but rather an attitude of mutual discovery and support of the team's growth.

The cooperation necessary for Future Capable Company teams is really more than cooperation; it is collaboration. Collaboration creates the synergy that drives a successful team. To begin the process of collaboration, the team should ask these questions:

- What can we do to foster a collaborative culture?
- How can we overcome individualism?
- How can we communicate our belief in collaboration?
- How can we begin the revolution toward collaboration right now?
- How will we celebrate our success?

Establish a Plan, Obtain Success, and Build on the Success

The fifth and sixth team-building steps result in the success needed to increase cooperation. This increases the team's strength and its ability to make increasingly significant improvements.

The seventh step is the positive reinforcement of the team's success. It is the end of one cycle in the Continuous Improvement process and the beginning of the next cycle. The team increases its commitment, dedication, and, therefore, its cooperation. In doing so, it becomes a collaborative unit that can be the basis for creating external collaboration and cooperation in the form of partnerships.

PARTNERSHIPS

At the rate that companies are banding together for various reasons, it is important to understand that only a specific type of partnership can create the external collaboration necessary for Continuous Improvement and thus, true Supply Chain Synthesis. Consider these definitions:

- When similar companies in the same kind of business band together to pool their resources to conduct research, evaluate technology, or lobby for a political position, they have not created a partnership, they have created a consortium.
- When companies lose their independence and become one corporate entity, it is not a partnership. It is an acquisition or merger.
- When companies work together to pursue a specific, single-focused business objective, this is not a partnership. It is a strategic alliance.
- When two companies form a separate entity with joint ownership to pursue a specific business objective, they have a joint venture, not a partnership.
- A long-term relationship based upon trust and a mutual desire to work together for the benefit of the other partner and the partnership is a true partnership.

Successful external collaboration for Continuous Improvement is achieved through the true partnership. That's because true partnerships are long-term collaborative relationships based on trust and a mutual desire to work together for the benefit of the other partner and the supply chain. The characteristics of a true partnership are:

- A commitment to long-term relationships based on trust and a true understanding of the partners' business.
- A belief in sharing information, planning, scheduling, risks, rewards, problems, solutions, and opportunities.
- A commitment to working together toward improvements in quality, lead-times, new product development time, and inventory accuracy and management.
- A resolution and agreement to build on each other's strengths, increase the partners' business, and invest in the long-term partnership relationship.
- A commitment to systems integration and organizational interdependence while still retaining individual identities to ensure

innovation and creativity.

- The consensus that frequent communications at all levels of the organization must occur and that partnership proximity is important and will be mutually addressed.
- A commitment to involving partners early in any innovations.
- A commitment to the flexibility required to ensure the best overall performance of the partnership.

Forming a true partnership requires discarding the traditional relationships common between organizations today. The objective of creating true partnerships is to create the same synergy between organizations that the collaboration process created within an organization. This means first understanding that the term "relationship" is not synonymous with partnership; instead, a relationship must be transformed into a partnership. This involves the following realizations:

- No two relationships develop the same way.
- Relationships evolve as comfortable bonds between individuals.
- A positive chemistry must exist between two parties to create a relationship.
- Partnerships evolve from understanding hopes and dreams, and anticipating a bright future.
- Each party must know itself and understand what it is seeking from the partnership.
- Acceptance by indirectly involved parties (e.g., stockholders, government) is as important to the perpetuation of the partnership as acceptance by directly affected parties.
- The relationship, at its core, has interest in the well-being of the other parties as well as the well-being of the partnership.
- Expectations of how the relationship will develop must be articulated.
- Compatibility is key to a long-term relationship.

Identifying potential true partners should be based on the opportunity for additional contribution to the growth and profitability of the supply chain. This applies to both a customer looking at its suppliers and a supplier looking at its customers. The focus should be on building trust, then communicating clearly, and, finally, adopting a Continuous Improvement process. As these relationships continue, the escalation of trust, openness, and success will naturally lead to sharing visions and strategic business plans and thus to Supply Chain Synthesis.

IDENTIFYING PARTNERS THROUGH ALLIANCES: CANDY CONTROLS AND DIEQUA

When Candy Controls landed a contract to upgrade printing press equipment, they knew which company could help them supply the specific shaft-phasing gearboxes required. It was its competitor in the printing and packaging market, Diequa of Bloomingdale, Illinois.

Candy had the electronics and the print registration system it needed. It did not have the gearboxes. The company knew that it would take an extensive amount of resources to design a new box, and that meant it might have missed the customer's deadline.

Diequa had off-the-shelf gearboxes that required no modifications. The companies agreed to work together, and to build trust into the relationship, they joined in a multiple-piece purchase. Their engineers worked together to provide a single proposal that the customer accepted.

Will they work together again? Candy Controls is moving toward electronic solutions where Diequa is not. As projects require the marriage of electronics and mechanical solutions, future relationships may develop. In other words, this successful alliance may be the foundation for Candy Controls' and Diequa's eventually forming a true partnership.

–Design News, August 21, 2000

As the partnership process evolves, a Partnership Initiative Team should be chartered. The purpose of this cross-functional team is to establish an official collaborative relationship, determine the objectives of the partnership, and develop a mutual plan for Supply Chain Synthesis. As a result, the identity of suppliers and customers will blur until the organizations are true partners. These partners will act as a synthesized supply chain to improve, grow, and prosper as Future Capable Companies, while maintaining their own corporate identities.

They have determined criteria for evaluating the partnerships, as well as potential new partners. Most importantly, they communicate with one another on causes of problems, on corrections, on improvement, and on the Continuous Improvement Success Path Forward that is the hallmark of Future Capable Companies and synthesized supply chains.

THE CONTINUOUS IMPROVEMENT SUCCESS PATH FORWARD

The Continuous Improvement Success Path Forward is the methodology for establishing continuous improvement once the collaboration and cooperation within and between supply chain organizations have been established. This path forward has the following steps:

1. Establish Continuous Improvement steering team and Continuous Improvement teams
2. Conduct customer and supplier roundtables
3. Define Continuous Improvement vision and evidence of success
4. Define prioritized opportunities for improvement
5. Implement Continuous Improvement team recommendations
6. Assess evidence of success
7. Define new prioritized opportunities for improvement
   The last sections of this chapter examine these steps.

Establish Continuous Improvement Steering Team and Continuous Improvement Teams

Continuous Improvement teams drive the Continuous Improvement process. For supply chain partners to achieve Continuous Improvement, they must use a Continuous Improvement steering team to create and charter many Continuous Improvement teams throughout the supply chain. Some of these teams will be cross-functional: they will address specific improvement opportunities with representatives across the supply chain. Others may address improvements in the organization of a specific partner. The members of the Continuous Improvement teams should be from broad cross-sections of the supply chain and should have demonstrated in the past that they are capable of achieving continuous improvements, breakthroughs, and innovation to enhance performance. The scope of each

Continuous Improvement team charter should be consistent with the knowledge of the members on the team and of sufficient focus to allow the team to achieve real performance improvements. It is critical that these teams meet as often as necessary to develop specific recommendations and plans of action to achieve peak performance in the areas that need improvement.

Develop a Continuous Improvement Business Plan

The Continuous Improvement steering team is responsible for developing a Continuous Improvement business plan. This should be a multiyear, macrolevel business plan that will define requirements for the future of the supply chain. It should be a set of goals and performance measures to ensure that all partners have a common view of the path forward. This will help the Continuous Improvement steering team and other leaders stay focused on continuous improvement. It also will help prepare them for changes in the supply chain and its requirements.

Conduct Customer and Supplier Roundtables

A roundtable is a meeting of peers for discussion and exchange of views. Customer and Supplier Roundtables should have representatives from throughout the supply chain, as well as from its ultimate consumers. The roundtables provide a facilitated opportunity for suppliers and customers to share ideas about products and markets interactively, query existing beliefs, and uncover new opinions.

The information collected from a Customer and Supplier Roundtable provides unique input into the development of a strategic plan for Continuous Improvement. The relationships they foster between customers and suppliers are invaluable. For example, participants are more clearly exposed to the complexity of supply chain relationships and become more confident as together they develop solutions from the roundtable questioning process.

Customer and Supplier Roundtables should be conducted regularly so supply chain members and the Continuous Improvement steering team are aware of changes in the supply chain. They also need to be ongoing. As each roundtable prepares follow-up questions, the answers to these questions must be addressed to strengthen the Continuous Improvement process.

Define Continuous Improvement Vision and Evidence of Success

A Continuous Improvement vision is not the doubletalk and doublethink so prevalent in American business today. Instead, as defined in my book *Revolution: Take Charge Strategies for Business Success*, it is: "A description of where you are headed." The Continuous Improvement vision should be stated so that the present is described as a past condition of the future, not as a future condition of the past. It should be expressions of optimism, hope, excellence, ideals, and possibilities for Continuous Improvement.

Define Prioritized Opportunities for Improvement

A benchmark assessment is a very useful tool in defining opportunities for Continuous Improvement. For example, an organization might evaluate its supply chain's current operations. Its total evaluation could then reveal that the target areas for improvement are customer satisfaction and manufacturing synthesis. The organization then focuses its Continuous Improvement efforts on the areas identified as weaknesses in the benchmark assessment (see Appendix A).

Implement Recommendations of the Continuous Improvement Teams

The improvement team's recommendations are to be shared with the steering team for review and approval. Once the steering team approves the recommendations, they should be implemented. The steering team should communicate the approved recommendations and remain committed to them throughout the implementation process.

Assess Evidence of Success

Those involved with the implementation of the Continuous Improvement team's recommendations and the Continuous Improvement steering team should maintain an ongoing record that tracks performance against the defined Evidence of Success. The record should be periodically reviewed to prioritize the next opportunities for improvement. The teams should then disseminate information about ongoing Continuous Improvements throughout the supply chain.

Define Newly Prioritized Opportunities for Improvement

Based on another benchmark conducted after the Evidence of Success shows that performance has improved, the steering team should prioritize the opportunities for the next iteration of the Continuous Improvement process. This is truly continuous improvement in action. Supply chain partners working together should never stop looking for ways to improve. They must lay down the same types of bricks in the path again and again if they wish to keep moving forward.

STAY ON THE PATH

Successful improvement implementations may not remain successful. Continuous Improvement is a dynamic process. Like a river, it is always moving. That means Future Capable Companies should move with it and make sure their Continuous Improvement efforts can keep up with the motion. The proper amount of internal and external cooperation and collaboration can achieve the process that will provide Future Capable Companies with the means for ensuring competitive advantage and meeting the Continuous Improvement Requirement of Success. The key is to stay on the Continuous Improvement Path Forward, ever searching for ways of improving relationships, processes, and products and focusing on synthesis, the last Requirement of Success for the Future Capable Company.

chapter 15

SYNTHESIS

T*he Future Capable Company must synthesize all functions. It must strive to achieve Supply Chain Synthesis by making sure that decisions are made in the context of the supply chain and the needs of the ultimate customer.*

Business and manufacturing boundaries and channels are merging and blurring. The vertical way of doing business—owning raw materials plants, manufacturing parts from them, assembling them, creating buffer stock from the assemblies, and shipping them to the warehouse—is undergoing tremendous change. Today's business consists of deverticalized companies and virtual factories that look to other companies for raw materials, manufacturing, distribution, and customer satisfaction. More and more companies are relying on alliances, partnerships, and similar collaborative efforts to produce products that delight the ultimate customer.

If companies are to succeed in these efforts and become Future Capable Companies, they must understand Supply Chain Synthesis (SCS). They must recognize that to deliver maximum value, customization, and satisfaction to the ultimate customer while at the same time reducing inventory, trimming lead-times, and reducing costs, the supply chain must become one entity. They must also synthesize their internal functions so they can lead their partners in the process that synthesizes the supply chain—SCS.

This chapter examines the process of SCS and presents its eight core competencies. It also demonstrates how a Future Capable Company can use SCS practices internally to ensure that decisions are made in the context of the supply chain and the needs of the ultimate customer.

SUPPLY CHAIN SYNTHESIS

SCS is a holistic, continuous improvement process of ensuring customer satisfaction from the original raw material provider to the ultimate, finished-product consumer. It melts the links in a supply chain into a smooth continuous flow. Visualize a river, properly banked and channeled, that is flowing toward a goal, and you are visualizing SCS. A river has no links, and although it comprises thousands of separate, natural forces, it is seen as one entity. Another way to look at it is to imagine a big chain passing over the flame of synthesis, the flame melting the chain and creating a flow of molten metal—SCS.

SCS presents significant opportunities. Implementing SCS will:

- Increase ROA through maximized inventory turns, minimized obsolete inventory, and maximized employee participation, and maximized continuous improvement.
- Improve customer satisfaction using customization, value-added activity, and flexibility to meet ever-changing customer requirements.
- Maximize speed through shorter response and lead-times and quick response to changes in the marketplace.
- Reduce costs through the scrutiny and analysis of all expenditures so that the lowest supply chain costs are achieved and then further reduced.
- Integrate the supply chain through partnerships and communication.

SCS has five main characteristics:

1. It is a well-defined process that is understood by all links along the supply chain. Those who practice SCS will see that it is important to consider every aspect of the supply chain and understand how each process fits, interacts, and integrates. Otherwise, critical information will be lost or an important link will be missing and all will be lost.

2. It is an integrated process in which selfishness is not allowed. This includes eliminating silos and focusing all links on customer satisfaction.

3. It is a process in which all involved understand the energy of change and have a desire to harness it for the competitive advantage of the total pipeline. This involves courage and innovation. By harnessing change, we can turn it into an asset for the total supply chain. Instead of thinking, "I want to improve my link," you may have to think, "Tradeoffs within my link might be what are needed to improve the supply chain."

4. It is a process that will not accept information delays. SCS requires true partnerships and an integration of information throughout the supply chain. If a link is slowing down information flow, it must be removed from the chain and replaced with an alternative.

5. It is process focused on achieving total supply chain performance excellence with specific performance criteria.

To make SCS happen, eight core competencies are required. They are:

1. Understanding Change
2. Understanding Peak-to-Peak Performance
3. Understanding Customer Satisfaction
4. Understanding Total Operations
5. Understanding Manufacturing Synthesis
6. Understanding Distribution Synthesis
7. Understanding SCS Partnerships
8. Understanding SCS Communications

It is important that a Future Capable Company master all eight core competencies and use them to synthesize the supply chain. Some of these competencies overlap the 12 Requirements of Success for the Future Capable Company. Change and Customer Satisfaction have already been discussed. Others correlate with them: Peak-to-Peak Performance and Partnerships are part of the continuous improvement process examined in Chapter 14, and Manufacturing Synthesis is key to achieving control and balance.

The rest of the competencies—Total Operations, Distribution Synthesis, and Communication—are critical to the success of the Future Capable Company.

TOTAL OPERATIONS

Total Operations integrates warehousing, logistics, manufacturing, quality, maintenance, organizational excellence, and systems. Total Operations does not focus on one technology or component. It is a holistic concept that stretches from planning a site through determining the correct network to the cultural ties that bind employees to an organization's mission. By focusing on the whole, a Total Operations view ensures an organization has:

- The correct distribution network
- The correct manufacturing methods
- The correct warehousing methods
- The correct operating systems
- The correct maintenance methods
- The quality to satisfy customers
- The correct process for Continuous Improvement

Total Operations is based on the premise that functions cannot be managed apart from all other operations in a company or a supply chain. This is because, in reality, everything affects operations: inbound and outbound transportation, material handling, preventive and predictive maintenance, statistical process control, manufacturing methods, customer satisfaction, inventory management, production planning, partnerships, teams, information, and warehousing methods. Therefore, pursuing Total Operations demands that:

- Distribution networks be designed from the perspective of the entire supply chain and not from the perspective of any one link. This may be achieved through Distribution Synthesis, which will be discussed in the next section.
- The proper manufacturing and warehousing methods be performed in the context of the whole supply chain. This includes warehousing and manufacturing practices driven by the correct operating systems—Warehouse Management Systems (WMS), Manufacturing Execution Systems (MES), Enterprise Asset Management (EAM), and Advanced Planning and Scheduling Systems (APS).
- The ultimate customer quality expectations be understood by all functions and links and be the driving force for defining maintenance and quality requirements. There must be an awareness of the customer, up and down, and along the entire supply chain, as well

as an awareness of the customer's definition of quality. Proper maintenance and quality methods and procedures must be in place to protect against breakdown and/or defective products that result in interruptions in service to the supply chain.

- All links understand the Continuous Improvement efforts of other links so the Continuous Improvement process focuses on the chain, and not the links. This prevents the sacrifice of one link to optimize another.

- The people throughout an organization and the supply chain be aligned and committed to the process of SCS. People truly enable synthesis—their attitudes, more than any other single factor, drive the success of Total Operations. If everyone involved in Total Operations is committed to satisfying the ultimate customer, everyone wins.

As these requirements demonstrate, Total Operations and SCS share similar goals with an ultimate destination—total integration. Both look at the whole through shared information and processes, so both add value to the whole. However, they have different scopes. That is why I usually recommend adopting Total Operations before adopting SCS. A Total Operations view prepares a company for SCS.

Distribution Synthesis

Distribution Synthesis is making sure that the right manufacturing operations and right distribution centers (DCs) are in the right locations and hold the right amount of inventory and that the right transportation is being used to fulfill the order to the satisfaction of the customer. When this is done from a link's perspective, it is called logistics. When it is done from a chain's perspective, the results are reduced inventory investments, reduced costs of distribution, improved customer satisfaction, and a streamlined flow of goods to the marketplace.

The characteristics of Distribution Synthesis include:
- Understanding the importance of customer requirements and satisfaction when designing a distribution network.
- A Distribution Strategic Master Plan that defines the requirements for an efficient and effective distribution system and includes a distribution network plan, a strategic warehouse master plan, and a transportation master plan.

- Proper utilization of Third Party Logistics.
- Economic and qualitative evaluation of all viable alternatives based on specific, weighted criteria before any distribution network decisions are made.
- Use of a hybrid push/pull system to maximize customer satisfaction and optimize manufacturing efficiency.

These characteristics generally define distribution synthesis for one organization. However, if a company has the knowledge to implement them internally, then that company has the knowledge to implement them for the entire supply chain. All distribution decisions (e.g., number and location of DCs, inventory levels, optimal order cycles and fulfillment rates, and order procedures) are then based on an SCS environment.

Communications

When an organization sets out to integrate business processes and disparate entities in the supply chain, there must be communication. It is vital to the success of all SCS core competencies. Today, organizations have a variety of options for communicating openly from direct links to virtual private networks, which transport data over secure Internet channels as if they were private lines. They also have a wide range of information systems available to them for strategic, tactical, and technical purposes.

These communication systems and options are radically changing today. Thanks to the Internet (and its most popular user interface, the World Wide Web), new partnerships and alliances are created almost daily because it inexpensively connects all means of communication together. Actually, there has been so much excitement over using the Internet to create B2B alliances and electronic trading communities that an important point is lost. The Internet can link countless suppliers, retailers, and customers, but if they don't use SCS communications, their partnerships and alliances will fail. The specific information systems used to perform these links are not important. What is critical is that the Internet be used as a vehicle for SCS communications, supporting SCS partnerships to achieve success.

SCS communication is simultaneous, instantaneous, and multi-directional so that everyone is working at the same time rather than sequentially. This eliminates inventory buffers and accelerates the flow of cash. It also allows dynamic planning, which replaces the outdated practices of long-term forecasting. It makes strategic information available to all partners so that all have contact with the customer and are aware of changing needs and trends. They can then respond in unison to these needs and trends.

SCS communications are clear, relevant, open, and honest. All parties are linked, and the information requirements of each are integrated into the communication process. That is why the Internet plays a key role in SCS communications. There are clear, concise, and ongoing communications at the outset as well as a willingness to share key information, withholding nothing, regardless of how close the relationship is. At the same time, there is a complete acceptance of the equality and interdependence of the players. Each has a leading role in one or more functional areas, no matter how they are interconnected. These basic communication principles are maintained throughout all supply chain processes.

Important to the success of SCS communications is the elimination of information silos. Information must be shared throughout the supply chain's communications network. SCS communications requires systems that can manage and transmit all types of data and information along the supply chain to ensure all partners receive accurate, timely, and high-quality information. It is critical that these systems exploit the power of the Internet to develop SCS communications.

Although Internet-linked information and communication systems are the most critical requirements for SCS communications, to be completely effective, they must also facilitate face-to-face and interpersonal communication to maintain the trust necessary for true information sharing and collaboration. This means intelligent participation in, and management of, person-to-person communication must be consistent with supply chain partner needs.

THE INTERNET AND COLLABORATION

Collaboration on a project, when all parties are in-house, has been going on for a long while. Now, the Internet makes it possible for engineers to collaborate

Continued

FUTURE CAPABLE COLLABORATION *Continued from page 167*

on a project from separate locations. The only drawback in providing real-time engineer-to-engineer collaboration is data-transfer speeds. Server-resident CAD programs meet with the greatest challenge where transfer speed is concerned because the designer must perform all operations online and through the variable speed of the company's particular Internet connection. Very high transfer speeds must be maintained for the collaboration to occur anywhere near real-time.

Through the use of local CAD software, Internet collaboration need only transfer those operations that have been completed, rather than the hand-shaking that goes on to manipulate a server-resident package. In this way, implementation speeds are much faster. Even this method can have its challenges. Often, special software add-ons have been created to facilitate online transfer of data through a variety of different hand-shaking schemes.

One company, Alibre, provides a web-based architecture with full 3D parametric, feature-based, associative solid modeling capabilities to the engineer. Key features of the software include the company's Real-Time Team Modeling, load-balanced distributed processing, and secure product data repository, sharing, and management capabilities.

–Design News, May 15, 2000

Building an SCS communications system requires integrating three essential types of capabilities. The system must be able to handle day-to-day communications and transactions along the supply chain, which can help align supply and demand because orders and daily schedules are shared. The system must also facilitate planning and decision-making, supporting demand and shipment planning necessary for distributing resources effectively. And finally, the system must provide tools such as an integrated network model that will allow strategic analysis. Electronic connectivity via the Internet provides the backbone for this communications system, which will greatly reduce transaction costs as orders, invoices, and payments are handled electronically and lower inventories through vendor-managed inventory programs. The key is ensuring the continuous flow of information.

SCS communication, distribution synthesis, and Total Operations, like the rest of the SCS core competencies, are not accomplished quickly and easily. It is best to start within an organization and work outward. I recommend that a Future Capable Company master all eight core competencies internally and, once mastered, use them to create a synthesized supply chain.

CREATING THE SYNTHESIZED SUPPLY CHAIN

Creating the synthesized supply chain involves design, planning, and execution. Supply chain design comprises network design, inventory design, transportation design, and customer satisfaction design. There is no single, best design for an integrated supply chain, but there are principles that can provide guidance for a Future Capable Company designing such a system with its supply chain partners. They should:

- View the supply chain design activity as an integrated process and appoint an SCS leader to oversee it
- Conduct regular sales and operations planning meetings that continuously review performance and operating concerns
- Operate with a single forecast and replenishment plan, not separate plans for finance, sales, logistics, and manufacturing
- Centralize process administration as well as the planning for inventory and replenishment requirements, but leave responsibility for forecasting and weekly/daily line scheduling close to the source
- Build flexibility into the system through SCS manufacturing, quick setup and changeover capabilities, cellular manufacturing, "postponement" principles, and a rapid and efficient planning cycle time
- Use decision-support tools, real-time information, and integrated software in the design process

Supply chain planning follows supply chain design. It is a detailed planning process created to meet the needs identified in the supply chain design process. It plans for the placement of the right materials at the right location at the right time. In many supply chain situations, the partners work well together on the design stage but become bogged down in the planning stage. This can happen for several reasons. First, they focus on software and not on synthesis. Supply chain partners must focus on results, using demand planning, event planning, inventory planning, replenishment planning, manufacturing planning, and transportation planning.

Demand planning is a method of forecasting based on past orders. Event planning is forecasting based on the future. Inventory planning identifies the optimal balance between inventory and desired levels of customer satisfaction based on industry's best practices. Replenishment planning determines the proper timing to achieve the inventory plan. Manufacturing planning involves the scheduling of the manufacturing operation, and transportation planning puts in place the procedures to bring the supply chain to life. These various components of supply chain planning must be linked and cumulative (e.g., demand planning and event planning should be used to drive inventory planning, which in turn should drive replenishment planning, etc.) for SCS to be achieved.

Supply chain execution is the final part of the process. Supply chain execution involves the systems that address SCS in real time: order management, warehouse management, transportation management, and manufacturing management. The Internet plays a role in the process as well—it is the means by which communications between supply chain planning and supply chain execution are accomplished. Order management accepts orders and passes them to the appropriate systems for fulfillment. Warehouse management supports the activities of the facility. Transportation management focuses on controlling costs and managing inbound, outbound, and intra-supply-chain goods movement. Manufacturing management ensures the efficiency and effectiveness of the manufacturing operations. Asset management is the maintenance of assets so that supply chain execution can occur without downtime created by unreliable equipment.

The results of supply chain execution affect supply chain planning because real-world events can change even the best-laid plans. It is good to review the supply chain planning components regularly and adjust them if execution warrants it. Supply chain planning in turn determines supply chain execution, and if it is altered, then the execution methods must also be altered.

During supply chain planning and execution, businesses must look outward. External applications—e-commerce, customer relationship management, and supply chains with industry-specific applications—are part of both. Supply chain planning and execution, therefore, require the following:

- A focus on the customer
- An acceptance of partnering
- An aggressive adaptation of technology, such as e-commerce
- A belief in the teaming process
- A focus on synchronized performance measures
- An openness to creativity and innovation
- A belief in the importance of having No Boundaries between the links of the chain

Creating a synthesized supply chain, then, requires an inward beginning and an outward growth. An organization that is synthesized internally and has used the correct processes to achieve that synthesis can then turn outward to the supply chain. Synthesis is the twelfth Requirement of Success for the Future Capable Company.

chapter 16

MAKING THE FUTURE CAPABLE COMPANY A REALITY

Future Capable Company is a manufacturing company that responds to the forces of change while using the proper application of technology. It not only focuses on the best solutions for today's requirements, it also focuses on the solution after next and moves from peak to peak to peak. A Future Capable Company also harnesses the power of change while integrating all manufacturing operations and applies technology for today's and tomorrow's requirements.

Transforming a company into a Future Capable Company requires patience, perseverance, and hard work. It means revolutionizing an organization and its supply chain. This means going beyond simple cultural changes and perceptions and transforming the rules, habits, procedures, standards, norms, rewards, language, jargon, stories, expectations, ceremonies, and titles that affect cultural conformance, organizational behavior, and organizational performance throughout the supply chain.

In other words, an organization cannot become a Future Capable Company overnight. The 12 Requirements of Success for the Future Capable are not easily met. However, with the total commitment of its leaders and employees, an organization can become a Future Capable Company and revolutionize its supply chain. How is this commitment achieved? Usually through one person, a Future Capable Company pioneer who has the Future Capable Company vision and makes the decision to spread this vision throughout an organization and its supply chain.

Spreading the vision means:

• Studying this book. It defines the Future Capable Company and its 12 Requirements of Success in detail and examines how the requirements can be met.
• Conducting a preliminary prioritization of the 12 Requirements of Success for the Future Capable Company.
• Communicating those Requirements of Success that have the highest priorities to management and other supply chain leaders.
• Motivating others, particularly organizational and supply chain leaders, to read this book by distributing it and scheduling a meeting to discuss it and the Future Capable Company vision.

Once organizational and supply chain leaders are aware of what a Future Capable Company is, the pioneer and others can schedule a meeting with two objectives:

1. Making sure that those at the meeting understand the 12 Requirements of Success for the Future Capable Company
2. Obtaining a commitment to transform the organization into a Future Capable Company

This commitment is a big step. It means all involved are on the same page and are ready to make big changes in the way they view and do business. It means that they realize that boundaries and channels are blurring, thanks to the sweeping changes of the last decade. They accept that business can no longer be contained in a huge factory that owns raw materials plants, manufactures parts from those raw materials, assembles them, creates buffer stock from the assemblies, and ships them to the warehouse. They embrace the idea of the virtual factory, with manufacturing functionalities existing in every link in the supply chain. They recognize that suppliers, manufacturers, and customers must cooperate and collaborate to survive in the war of supply chain vs. supply chain by practicing SCS, the holistic, continuous improvement process of ensuring customer satisfaction from the original raw material provider to the ultimate, finished-product consumer.

In this book, I have discussed the changing nature of business-to-business and business-to-consumer relationships and how they are affecting manufacturing. I outlined what being a Future Capable Company means, introduced the 12 Future Capable Company Requirements for Success, discussed how to achieve each of the 12 Requirements, and identified the path forward for the Future Capable Company.

Those who have made the commitment to transform their company into a Future Capable Company must be willing to work hard to achieve success. If they apply the knowledge within this book, the transformation will be both smooth and successful. I wish you well as you begin your journey to becoming a Future Capable Company.

SCS
BENCHMARK
ASSESSMENT

The following nine tables represent a
version of an assessment tool to conduct
the nine-point audit of the Supply Chain
Synthesis Benchmark Assessment.

FIRST AUDIT POINT OF SCS—SUPPLY CHAIN HEALTH

Action Item	1=Strongly Disagree		3=Agree		5=Strongly Agree
The supply chain process in the organization is well-defined and understood by all members of the supply chain.	1	2	3	4	5
There is not pervasive siloism within the supply chain; that is, supply chain members do not focus on self-optimization rather than optimization of the whole.	1	2	3	4	5
All supply chain links focus on customer satisfaction.	1	2	3	4	5
Information delays are not tolerated.	1	2	3	4	5
All supply chain members understand that change cannot be managed, only harnessed.	1	2	3	4	5
The supply chain has true and open partnerships that share information readily and expeditiously.	1	2	3	4	5
The competitive advantage of the entire pipeline is more important than the competitive advantage of each member of the pipeline.	1	2	3	4	5

Total Score This Section: _____

SECOND AUDIT POINT OF SCS—CHANGE

Action Item	1=Strongly Disagree		3=Agree		5=Strongly Agree
Each employee has clearly defined responsibilities, accountabilities, roles, and identities.	1	2	3	4	5
There is continuity in the purpose of the organization.	1	2	3	4	5
Expectations of each employee are delineated and only altered after conference and mutual agreement.	1	2	3	4	5
Everyone understands the necessity of change.	1	2	3	4	5
All employees believe that change will benefit them both personally and professionally.	1	2	3	4	5
The focus of employees within the organization is consistent with the focus of the organization itself.	1	2	3	4	5
Organizational focus is proactively, rather than reactively, maintained.	1	2	3	4	5
Employees are encouraged to participate in and provide feedback to organizational changes.	1	2	3	4	5
Information flows through the organization in a timely manner.	1	2	3	4	5

Total Score This Section: _____

THIRD AUDIT POINT OF SCS—PEAK-TO-PEAK PERFORMANCE

Action Item	1=Strongly Disagree		3=Agree		5=Strongly Agree
Peak performance is often the beginning of failure.	1	2	3	4	5
The organization is striving to evolve from a succeed/fail organization to a succeed/succeed one.	1	2	3	4	5
The organization needs to install processes that anticipate and solve problems before they are problems.	1	2	3	4	5
Continuous renewal is important in Peak-to-Peak Performance.	1	2	3	4	5
There will always be more problems than solutions.	1	2	3	4	5
The organization needs to solve problems by thinking "outside the box" and reaching to a level that is beyond the problem.	1	2	3	4	5
A shift to a process of continuously changing paths is required for Peak-to-Peak Performance.	1	2	3	4	5
Success only buys a ticket to higher-level problems.	1	2	3	4	5

Total Score This Section: _____

Fourth Audit Point of SCS—Total Operations

Action Item	1=Strongly Disagree		3=Agree		5=Strongly Agree
The correct distribution network and logistics methods are in place to provide product at the right place at the right time in the most cost-effective manner.	1	2	3	4	5
Operational efficiency is assured through the correct manufacturing and warehousing methods, resources, and processes.	1	2	3	4	5
Proper procedures are in place to protect against equipment breakdown and malfunction.	1	2	3	4	5
The quality control system provides the organization with tools necessary to reduce and even eliminate defects from our products.	1	2	3	4	5
There is adequate buffer to allow interruptions in service.	1	2	3	4	5
There is a process to assure continuous improvement in our operations.	1	2	3	4	5
There is a process to assure continuous improvement in our pipeline (i.e. partnerships and alliances).	1	2	3	4	5
The organization takes advantage of SCS and Total Operations to capture the energy of change.	1	2	3	4	5

Total Score This Section: _____

181

FIFTH AUDIT POINT OF SCS—CUSTOMER SATISFACTION

Action Item	1=Strongly Disagree		3=Agree		5=Strongly Agree
The organization believes that de-massification of product, rather than mass production, will be a driver of exemplary customer satisfaction.	1	2	3	4	5
The customer is the co-creator of value.	1	2	3	4	5
Ongoing customer dialogue is key to success.	1	2	3	4	5
Sharing of minds and wallets is more important than retention.	1	2	3	4	5
My organization is finding that sales and service are merging.	1	2	3	4	5
It is good business to treat customers as individuals rather than as demographics.	1	2	3	4	5
Customer segmentation based on order quantities and % of profit is a route to SCS.	1	2	3	4	5
Customer satisfaction issues impact more than product quality and service.	1	2	3	4	5

Total Score This Section: _____

SIXTH AUDIT POINT OF SCS—MANUFACTURING SYNTHESIS

Action Item	1=Strongly Disagree		3=Agree		5=Strongly Agree
Leadership understands that significant lead time reduction must occur.	1	2	3	4	5
The only way to maintain manufacturing efficiency while reducing production lot sizes is to reduce setup times.	1	2	3	4	5
The organization realizes that balancing a series of operations is more important than the speed of any of those operations.	1	2	3	4	5
The facility consists of focused departments that provide balance and support for manufacturing.	1	2	3	4	5
No one in manufacturing over- or under-produces.	1	2	3	4	5
WIP buffers are installed only when sequential flow cannot be achieved.	1	2	3	4	5
All uncertainty is minimized in manufacturing, and discipline increased since there is insufficient time to deal with unplanned and untimely events.	1	2	3	4	5
All operations are performed according to communicated, well-defined standards.	1	2	3	4	5

Total Score This Section: _____

SEVENTH AUDIT POINT OF SCS—DISTRIBUTION SYNTHESIS

Action Item	1=Strongly Disagree		3=Agree		5=Strongly Agree
The organization understands the importance of customer requirements and satisfaction when designing a distribution network.	1	2	3	4	5
Third party logistics (3PL) providers are often used in peak demand times to improve financial performance (i.e. replace seasonally utilized DCs).	1	2	3	4	5
The company has a Distribution Strategic Master Plan (DSMP), which defines the requirements for an efficient and effective distribution system.	1	2	3	4	5
The organization uses Leadership Roundtables early in the design of a distribution network to develop ideas about new products, customer requirements, technologies, and sourcing of materials.	1	2	3	4	5
All distribution decisions (e.g., number and location of DCs, inventory levels, optimal order cycles and fulfillment rates, and order procedures) are based in an SCS, rather than SCM (or even traditional logistics), environment.	1	2	3	4	5
Forecasting is not used in determining distribution requirements.	1	2	3	4	5
The organization uses a hybrid system of distribution to maximize customer satisfaction and optimize manufacturing efficiency.	1	2	3	4	5
Before any distribution network decisions are made, all viable alternatives are economically and qualitatively evaluated based on specific, weighted criteria.	1	2	3	4	5

Total Score This Section: _____

EIGHTH AUDIT POINT OF SCS—PARTNERSHIPS

Action Item	1=Strongly Disagree		3=Agree		5=Strongly Agree
The organization believes that the challenges one faces in partnerships (e.g. trust, communications, and culture) must be overcome to secure competitive advantage.	1	2	3	4	5
Improved performance of the TOTAL pipeline is necessary through partnerships.	1	2	3	4	5
The keys to partnership success are: integration, information, and interaction.	1	2	3	4	5
The organization is communicating with supply chain members on causes of problems, corrections, and continuous improvement, rather than on the problems themselves.	1	2	3	4	5
The days of "carrot and stick" vendor relationships are over.	1	2	3	4	5
The organization understands the importance of sharing information on sales and purchasing trends with its supply chain.	1	2	3	4	5
The organization chooses its partners based on both quantitative and qualitative criteria that specifically address strategic needs.	1	2	3	4	5
It is important to benchmark partnership activity for continuous improvement.	1	2	3	4	5

Total Score This Section: _____

185

Ninth Audit Point of SCS—Communications

Action Item	1=Strongly Disagree		3=Agree		5=Strongly Agree
Managing and communicating information to supply chain partners is vital to organizational success.	1	2	3	4	5
Information and communications systems are different entities.	1	2	3	4	5
The organization's communications systems enable sharing of a wide variety of information forms.	1	2	3	4	5
The future of the supply chain communications systems is "e."	1	2	3	4	5
The organization is investing in technologies that facilitate information sharing through secure means.	1	2	3	4	5
All supply chain members use a variety of strategic, tactical, and technical information systems.	1	2	3	4	5
A homegrown legacy system is not the best example of how information can be shared through SCS communications.	1	2	3	4	5
The organization is comfortable with sharing enterprise information with its partners.	1	2	3	4	5

Total Score This Section: _____

EVALUATING CURRENT OPERATIONS

After assessing each of the elements of SCS, you should assess the total scope of your operations as well. Write down the figures for each of the nine areas in the spaces provided below.

	Rating	Target Rating
Supply Chain "Health"		35
Change		45
Peak-to-Peak		40
Total Operations		40
Customer Satisfaction		40
Manufacturing Synthesis		40
Distribution Synthesis		40
Partnerships		40
Communications		40
TOTAL		360

Rating ÷ Target Rating = _____%

A+	**Excellent**	**97% and higher**
A	**Very Good**	**90 – 96.99%**
B	**Good**	**80 – 89.99%**
C	**Average**	**75 – 79.99%**
C-	**Below Average**	**70 – 74.99%**
D	**Poor**	**Less than 70%**

For example, Forsyth Widgets, Inc. has evaluated each of
the core requirements for SCS based on its current operations.
Its total evaluation, when placed in table form, reveals the following:

	Rating	Target Rating
Supply Chain "Health"		35
Change		45
Peak-to-Peak		40
Total Operations		40
Customer Satisfaction		40
Manufacturing Synthesis		40
Distribution Synthesis		40
Partnerships		40
Communications		40
TOTAL		360

Rating ÷ Target Rating = _____ %

A score of 255/360 = 71%, or C- (below average). This should be an
indicator to the company that many areas of SCS require responsive
and comprehensive re-envisioning; success within the supply chain
cannot happen otherwise. The next step should be investigating each
criterion and determining specific courses of action.

AUDIT ITEMS COMPARED

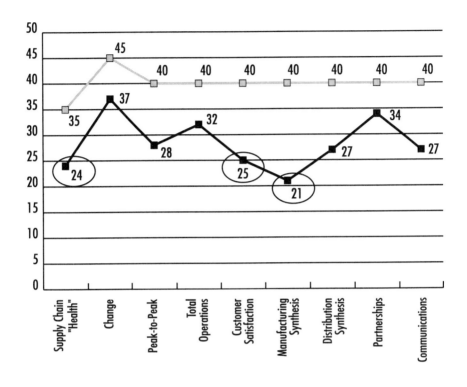

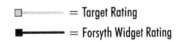
= Target Rating
= Forsyth Widget Rating

WORKS CONSULTED

Anderson, Cheri. "LucasVarity Goes World Class." *Assembly*, June 1999.

Casselman, Grace. "The New eSupply Chain." *ebiz*, Vol. 2, No. 3.

Feare, Tom. "Keeping Assembly Simple." *Modern Materials Handling,* Jan. 1, 2000.

Feare, Tom. "Tracking Space-Bound Materials for Earth Assembly." *Modern Materials Handling*, May 1, 2000.

"Focused Factory: Continental Teves." *Automotive Manufacturing and Production*, July 2000.

(*Fortune*, date unknown)

Hill, Sidney. "Adexa: A New Name and New Approach for a New Era." *MSI Magazine*, February 2000.

Koelsch, James R. "Torque It Tight; Torque It Right." *Assembly*, September 2000.

Koshio, Soichi. "No Global Strategy Without Information Sharing." *Design News*, Sept. 20, 1999.

Ogando, Joseph. "Diet by Design." *Design News*, Jan. 17, 2000.

Owen, Terry. "Not Flowing Around." *MSI Magazine,* April 2000.

Persun, Terry. "Online Engineering Collaboration." *Design News*, May 15, 2000.

Reich, Robert. "Your Job Is Change." *The American Prospect Online,* Aug. 21, 2000.

Russelburg, Kevin. "Partners in Design." *Design News*, Aug. 21, 2000.

Sprovieri, John. "A Close Look at Assembly." *Assembly,* September 2000.

Stein, Nicholas. "Measuring People Power." *Fortune*, Oct. 2, 2000.

"The Dogfood Danger." *The Economist*, April 6, 2000.

Tompkins, James A. *No Boundaries: Moving Beyond Supply Chain Management*. Raleigh, N.C.: Tompkins Press, 2000.

Tompkins, Jim. *Revolution: Take Charge Strategies for Business Success*. Raleigh, N.C.: Tompkins Press, 1998.

Weber, Austin. "Big Trucks = Big Profits." *Assembly*, June 2000.

Wingo, Walter. "CEN Develops Global Strategy for Luer Connection Problems." *Global Design News*, June 1, 2000.

Wyle, Charles. "Medical device Assembly: Phased-In Automation." *Assembly*, January 1999.

INDEX

A

Adaptability, 61, 78, 83, 85, 122
Advance shipping notice (ASN), 48
Alibre, 168
Alper, William, 138
American Society for Quality, 109, 110
Americans with Disabilities Act, 128
Annual usage, 74
Anticipated cost-reduction performance, 40
Apple Computer, 8
ARPANET, 1
Aspect Development Inc., 13
Atlas Copco Tools Inc., 113
Automation, 85

B

B2B2B2B2B, 14, 19, 20, 21
B2B2B2B2B2C, 12, 15, 16, 17, 20, 21
Bedrocks, 28
Blurred boundaries, 24
BMW, 53
Bosack, Len, 26
BP Amoco, 137

Buckingham, Marcus, 142
Build-to-Order (BTO), 4, 5, 65, 66, 67
Business-to-business (B2B), 11, 12, 13, 14, 15, 16, 17, 21, 166
Business-to-consumer (B2C), 11, 12, 15, 21, 150

C

Cahners Business Information, 13
Candy Controls, 156
Cannondale, 36
Capacity Constraining Resources (CCR), 91
Cease-fire, 45, 46, 47
CERN, 1
Chambers, John, 26, 65
Change, 2, 3, 7, 17, 18, 19, 23, 24, 25, 26, 28, 29, 30, 33, 34, 42, 47, 57, 61, 67, 68, 69, 70, 71, 76, 77, 78, 80, 81, 82, 83, 86, 89, 93, 136, 140, 149, 161, 163, 170, 173, 179, 192
Cisco Systems, 26, 27, 28, 65
Clarke, Arthur C., 1
Coca-Cola, 53
Coffman, Curt, 142
Collaboration, 138, 150, 151, 153, 154, 155, 157, 160, 167, 168, 192

193